THE BOOK
OF LISTS

THE BOOK OF LISTS

IAN MESSITER

THE LIST OF LISTS

Orchestral instruments **15**
London school children's languages **16**
Ten terrible tongue twisters **17**
A short Franz Liszt (1811-1886) **17**
Odd explosions **18**
Things dating couples argue about **19**
A list of palindromes **20**
A shrt lst of od wrds **20**
How to say 'Hello' **21**
Popular misconceptions **22**
Unusual collective terms **23**
The seven wonders of the world **24**
Wedding anniversaries **25**
'My ten greatest comedians' from Bob Monkhouse **25**
Ten towns that failed the EEC beach pollution test **26**
Ten towns that passed the EEC pollution test **27**
A list of gardens **27**
How to address royalty **28**
Angels in descending order of rank **29**
How to address the Clergy **30**
Helpful hints on preparing a second hand car for sale **31**
A list of colours and what they might mean to those who wear them to excess **32**
Frequent misquotations **34**
A booze news list **34**
Unsolicited mail found on my hall mat **35**

Bob Monkhouse lists 'My ten worst puns' 37
100 people were asked 'What do you want out of life above all else?' 38
Squid facts 38
Main causes of road accidents 39
Fictitious detectives 40
Names that have been or are still registered trade names 41
Alcohol proof systems 41
British born inventors 42
Travellers' last minute panics 43
A list of futilities 44
Ten frequently told lies 45
A list of clichés 46
The ten most used words in this book 47
Animals in Chinese years 47
Famous remarks 48
A list from astronomer Patrick Moore 49
A list about Patrick Moore 50
Cocktails from three masters of the art 50
Events during the building of Nelson's column in Trafalgar Square 52
A list about Angela Willans 53
Ten most frequent problems from Angela Willans 53
Memorable occasions in the history of flight 54
The eight major religions 55
A list of boxers from Henry Cooper OBE, KSG 56
Nine references to a gentleman 57
Downstairs and upstairs with Margaret Powell 58
100 people asked to name a bad luck superstition they <u>believed</u> in said this 59
Names which have changed 59
Ten common tautological expressions 60

Ten words you are unlikely to have met before 60
Five strange things from the sea 61
Words often confused 62
Phrase origins 63
A list of crazed phrase 64
Reasons to stop smoking 64
Ways to stop smoking 66
Male and female differences 66
Notable dates in space exploration 68
Birthstones and flowers 69
Some of the morals of Aesop's fables 70
Reasons for sleeplessness 70
Ten ways to save petrol 71
The cost of a railway ticket 72
The seven sages 72
Patron saints 73
Hippo facts 74
Interesting happenings in 1884 75
Left overs 76
Words etcetera 76
Words with their origins in names 77
Facts about your skin 78
Words most used in conversation 78
Ten printed items that made me laugh 79
Real but sometimes unfortunate names of people 80
Biblical forties 80
Words often used incorrectly 81
Odd mammal facts 82
Eleven cities furthest by air from the UK 83
A list about the lie detector 83
Coal prices 84
The ten most popular package deal continental holiday
resorts 84

Our solar system planets **85**
Place names that do not look as they sound **87**
Weekday births according to old superstition **88**
Seven deadly sins **88**
Ten old and still popular indoor games **88**
UK caves worth visiting **90**
A UK numerical place names list **91**
Mazes and labyrinths **92**
Ten remarkable castles **92**
The ten longest rivers in round figures **94**
Drivers' statements after an accident **94**
A list of fatal accidents **96**
Feminist proposals **96**
World times **97**
Ornithological oddities **98**
Unusual UK place names **99**
Words found on some menus **100**
Bishops' signatures **103**
Your character from your food **104**
Strange facts about some people **104**
Vegetation which can be used to make wine **106**
Facts about the Taj Mahal **107**
We stopped 100 ladies in London's Oxford Street and
asked them what they thought was the most difficult item
to iron **108**
Ways to be a wally **109**
Simpson's-in-the-Strand (London) menu **110**
Things you could buy for an old penny **110**
Twelve signs of the zodiac **111**
Seven champagne bottle sizes **113**
Horible happenings of 100 years ago (1884) **114**
Haggis ingredients **115**
Information about Halley's Comet **116**

Facts about the world's most venomous snake **117**
A list of money terms which often confuse **118**
Regretted statements **120**
Eight reasons to eat garlic **121**
Paired words that sound wrong when reversed **122**
A list of Chinese interest **122**
If you are superstitious do not read this unlucky thirteen list **124**
Twelve famous last words **125**
A list of ten languages **126**
The nine muses **126**
100 people named dogs they fear most **127**
Occult beliefs **128**
A list for migraine sufferers **129**
A list of parlour games great-grandmother played **130**
Camel facts **133**
Hiccup cures **134**
A list of fallacies **134**
A list of radio comedy greats **136**
Rules for life **141**
Stars thought to wear wigs **142**
Fishy facts **142**
Things done for five minutes **144**
Famous mysteries **144**
English place names and their Roman counterparts **146**
Vogue words **147**
Animals originally foreign to our shores but now naturalized **148**
Nicholas Parson's list of eleven exciting batsmen **150**
My list of curious musical instruments **151**
A list of threes **153**
Items handed in to Heathrow lost property office **153**
A list of wrong names **154**

Somnolent themes **155**
Curious health facts **156**
Unmusical items which have been used as musical
instruments **157**
Items stolen by office workers **158**
A crazy alphabet list **159**
Things done in five minutes **159**
Common expressions and how we came by them **160**
A list of all rights **161**
Some first names with their origins — are you here? **163**
A remarkable list from the Guinness Book of Records **169**
Classic magic tricks **172**
Magicians and conjurors **173**
A Christmas list **176**
A list of Smiths **177**
Accidents **179**
A curious list of things people have done for no apparent
reason **179**
Japanese monster films **181**
Eating and drinking records **181**
Landmarks in the advent of the computer **182**
Origins of words **184**
A handy list of weights and measures **186**
A list mainly of epitaphs **188**

INTRODUCTION

What makes a list? There are no rules. It could, for example, be a catalogue of newspaper mistakes, beginning with these classified ads: 'Parents of the Newborn Babies' Club will hold their weekly meetings on Saturdays at 4.00 a.m.', followed by 'The Society of Crystal Gazers have had to cancel their usual Wednesday meeting due to unforeseen circumstances.' You have only to scan the papers to find plenty more but, such is the nature of list-making, that you will probably get diverted from this trail to follow the tracks of many new lists before returning to the original. To get you started, here is a list of words that do not rhyme with any others: ORANGE, SILVER, CHIMNEY, CARPET, LIQUID, WINDOW, SPIRIT and PURPLE. Can you add to it? And while we're on the subject, here's a list of words that have changed their meanings over the centuries: today NICE means PLEASING, but its original meaning was EXACT; SILLY once meant HOLY; PANTOMIME originally was a dumb show and therefore included ballet in its scope; PECULIAR at one time had the meaning 'special to a particular person' and thence came to mean DIFFERENT or STRANGE.

The fascinating thing about lists is that, not only does the compiling of them constantly suggest new ideas, but also the mere grouping of facts or ideas for one reason will often result in another set of interesting comparisons within the same list. Hence you will find a huge diversity of subjects amongst those offered here, together with much illuminating behind-the-scenes information.

Practically everyone makes lists, of course. Take the shopping list for example. It may not make such interesting reading now, but one made a hundred years ago would be fascinating. So before you turn the pages to discover what an intriguing kaleidoscope of lists and ideas have been set out with the sole purpose of delighting you, why not resolve to keep a copy of your next shopping list? Lock it in your bank with the instruction that no one shall read it for a thousand years.

In writing this book I have had many generous, if not always practical, suggestions for lists from all sorts of people. One good friend urged that I should include a list of Members of Parliament who went to bed with their socks on, but wasn't so keen on carrying out the necessary survey of the 600 odd MPs.

Doctor Johnson said that a man would turn over half a library to make one book. This book could only have been assembled by turning over a whole library if it had not been for the invaluable help given me by the many friends listed. My thanks to them all.

The List of Outside Contributors

JOHN ACKLEY for his strange list of reasons for accidents as written on motorists' insurance claims.

BOB BURTON, RITZ HEAD BARTENDER for his list of cocktails.

CHARLES CHILTON for his contribution to humorous quotes.

R. L. CLARKE OBE of the BRITISH BOXING BOARD OF CONTROL for his detailed research of fighters.

HENRY COOPER OBE, KSG for his list of great fighters.

T. J. EDGINGTON, Information Officer of the National Railway Museum, York, for his research on the prices of rail tickets from London to Birmingham.

A. R. FAIRLIE of 'THE HOWTOWDIE' Edinburgh for his list of cocktails.

TONY FRAY, BERKELEY HOTEL, HEAD BARTENDER, for his list of cocktails.

LYN AND KATE GOLDBERG for their list of odd place names.

ALEX GREENE OF THE R. A.C. for his list of the main causes of road accidents.

BOBBY JAYE, HEAD OF LIGHT ENTERTAINMENT BBC RADIO, RICHARD EDIS, RADIO PRODUCER, MARC PLATT, PROGRAMME INDEX DEPT., YOLANDE HARNIESS, BBC DATA, for the list of radio comedy greats.

PAUL LEGG of BARCLAY TRUST for his list of fiscal terms.

MY WIFE, ENID, for suggesting some useful lists.

CHRISTINE MESSITER, my daughter-in-law, for her list of unusual instruments.

MALCOLM MESSITER, my son, for his list of orchestral instruments.

BOB MONKHOUSE for his list of great comedians and for his list of worst puns.

PATRICK MOORE for his list of astonishing facts about the universe.

NICHOLAS PARSONS for his list of cricketers.

THE LATE MARGARET POWELL for her list of emotions.

J. A. SPIEGEL, MANAGING DIRECTOR OF CHARRINGTON'S SOLID FUEL LTD for his list of coal prices since 1890.

ANGELA WILLANS, 'AGONY AUNT' OF WOMAN'S OWN, for her list of readers' problems.

M. C. WILLIAMS, GENERAL MANAGER OF SIMPSON'S-IN-THE-STRAND, LONDON, for his list of menu prices since a long time ago.

PATTI WHITE of A. S. H. for her reasons to stop smoking and for her list of ways to give up smoking.

KATHERINE WHITEHORN for her contribution to the humorous quotations.

The lists from The Guinness Book of Records ('A remarkable list'; 'A curious list of things people have done for no apparent reason' and 'Eating and drinking records') are copyright and published by kind permission of Guinness Superlatives Limited.

First published in Great Britain in 1984 by Octopus Books Limited
59 Grosvenor Street
London W1

© 1984 Hennerwood Publications Limited

ISBN 0 86273 125 9

Printed and bound in Great Britain by Collins, Glasgow

Illustrations by Tom Johnston

THE LISTS

Orchestral instruments

This list was supplied by Malcolm Messiter, himself an oboe virtuoso. There is no end to the objects that can be used as musical instruments, so this list is confined to those expected in a normal orchestra. There is no set size for an orchestra which can vary from 20 to more than 100.

1. **WOODWINDS** from large to small. The Bassoon, the Cor Anglais, the Clarinet, the Oboe, the Flute and the Piccolo. The last two, although classed as woodwind, are today frequently made of metal. All the above can be made of plastic with varying degrees of success.
2. **THE BRASS WIND INSTRUMENTS** are the Tuba, the Horn, the Trombone and the Trumpet. They are usually called simply 'the brass' and are mostly made from that metal although there are many exceptions.
3. **STRINGED INSTRUMENTS** are played with a bow and are more usually known as 'the strings'. They are, from large to small, the Double Bass, the Cello, the Viola and the Violin. As with the woodwinds, these too have been copied in plastic and with varying degrees of failure. The only stringed instrument not played with a bow is the Harp, and there are at least 5 types of these apart from the familiar upright type with pedals.
4. **PERCUSSION INSTRUMENTS** are those that are struck to produce a sound. There is a large variety of these, so here are the usual ones. The Bass Drum, the Tenor Drum, the Snare Drum, the Side Drum, the Kettle Drum, the Tambourine, the Cymbals, the Tubular Bells and the Triangle. Because it is struck to produce a sound, the piano is sometimes called a percussion instrument.

   Those are the basics of an orchestra to which are often added these familiar sound makers, the Xylophone, the Concertina, the Harmonica or Mouth-organ, the Sousaphone and, last but not least, for the 1812, the Cannon.

London school children's languages

Within the Inner London Education Authority's schools an astonishing 147 languages are spoken. The twelve most common in descending order of popularity are:

1. ENGLISH
2. BENGALI
3. TURKISH
4. GUJERATI
5. SPANISH
6. GREEK
7. URDU
8. PUNJABI
9. CHINESE
10. ITALIAN
11. ARABIC
12. FRENCH

Ten terrible tongue twisters

Most can be said once with ease, but try repeating them six times.

1. Six twin screwed steel steam cruisers.
2. The Leith police dismisseth us.
3. She sells sea shells beside the sea shore.
4. The crow flew over the river with a lump of raw liver.
5. Preshrunk silk shirts.
6. 'Are you copperbottoming 'em my man?' 'No'm. I'm aluminiuming 'em, mum.'
7. A bloke's bike back brake block broke.
8. Mixed biscuits.
9. She stood by Burgess's fish-sauce shop welcoming him in.
10. Tie twine to three tree twigs.

Tongue twisters have a curious history. At various times they have been thought to be: a cure for hiccups; a cure for lisping; a test for radio announcers; a test for sobriety and a test for false teeth.

A short Franz Liszt (1811-1886)

1. Aged nine he first appeared in public in Odenburg. He was so excellent that several noblemen guaranteed his finance for six years' study.
2. He wrote twenty one orchestral works.
3. . . . and seven for piano and orchestra of which some were based on works by other composers, such as his Fantasia on themes from Beethoven's 'Ruins of Athens'.
4. . . . and ninety six piano solos,
5. . . . and two arrangements for two pianos,
6. . . . and two pieces for piano and violin,
7. . . . and nine compositions for organ or harmonium,
8. . . . and twenty one masses, psalms and other sacred music,
9. . . . and nine for men's voices only,
10. . . . and over eighty other musical pieces as well as nine literary works, some of which include musical illustrations.

It is said that when a guest at the Vatican he was the only man allowed by the Pope to have a mistress living with him.

Odd explosions

1. **The case of the exploding whale.** The corpse of a fifty foot long whale was washed up on a Lincolnshire beach in the mid 1970s. While the authorities were discussing the best way to dispose of it, the problem solved itself. The whale exploded.

2. **Diamonds are not always for ever.** Freshly mined diamonds are likely to explode and sometimes they do.
3. **Exploding ivory.** Refrigerated elephants' tusks, if not thawed out slowly, will explode.
4. **Lobsters can't stand the pressure.** Live lobsters flying at heights above 600 metres (2,000 feet) will explode. (You are entitled to ask what live lobsters are doing flying at any height. The answer is that an enterprising Scot caught lobsters off the west coast and sold them to the expensive restaurants in the south of France. The condition of delivery was that they must be alive. So, packed in wet bladderwrack seaweed, he flew them. Leaving the relatively high pressure under water for the low pressure at 600 metres (2,000 feet) they exploded and splattered themselves all around the aircraft.)

5. **Not-so-harmless milk.** The dust of dried milk has been known to explode, demolishing an entire warehouse.
6. **Explosive fumes.** Ivan Stobb was a Russian alcoholic in Moscow in the 1950s. He blew himself up after drinking a large quantity of neat vodka when he tried to light a cigarette.
7. **Out like a light.** (Unsubstantiated) A vicar in Dorset blowing out the altar candles exploded and died instantly.
8. **The biggest ever.** The greatest explosion in human history was that of Krakatoa, a volcano between Java and Sumatra, on August 27, 1883.
9. **Beware the exploding gourd.** There is a gourd which grows from a 'dynamite' tree in Mexico. When ripe, the gourd explodes with such violence that the hard, jagged splinters can kill.
10. **The start of it all.** Perhaps the strangest explosion of all is the 'Big Bang' theory which created the universe. It is said that the bang is still expanding, but one day will reverse itself.

Things dating couples argue about

The interviews were conducted at a busy shopping centre on two days during the last week of October 1983.

1. **34%** said they argued about where to go.
2. **18%** said they argued about money.
3. **16%** said, after a few giggles, they argued about sex.
4. **8%** said they argued about time keeping. It seems the man was usually the one to be late most often.
5. **6%** said they argued about jealousy.
6. **6%** said they argued about the kind of wedding they would have.
7. **2%** said they argued about their parents.
8. **2%** said they argued about where to live.
9. **2%** said they argued about what film to see.
10. One couple only said they never argued.

There are a few couples missing as you will see if you add up the percentages. This is because they said they argued but could not remember what about.

A list of palindromes

A palindrome is a word or sentence that can be read either way.

1. ABLE WAS I ERE I SAW ELBA.
2. MADAM, I'M ADAM.
3. REDIVIDER (The longest palindromic English word.)
4. I ROAMED UNDER IT AS A TIRED NUDE MAORI.
5. A MAN, A PLAN, A CANAL — PANAMA!
6. WAS IT A CAR OR A CAT I SAW?
7. WON'T LOVERS REVOLT NOW?
8. LIVE NOT ON EVIL.
9. PA'S A SAP.
10. STAR RATS.
11. TRAP PART IF I TRAP PART.
12. DOGS A DEVIL DEIFIED, DEIFIED LIVED AS GOD.

And as a finale, here is the world's longest palindrome.
It is in Latin:
13. ODO TENET MULUM, MADIDAM MAPPAM TENET ANNA, ANNA
    TENET MAPPAM MADIDAM, MULUM TENET ODO.

In English it means ODO HOLDS A MULE, ANNA HOLDS A WET DRIPPING NAPKIN, ANNA HOLDS A WET DRIPPING NAPKIN, ODO HOLDS A MULE, which is about as sensible as those Latin sentences we learned at school, such as 'I love a table', 'They love a table'.

A shrt lst of od wrds

1. INCOMPLET
2. MISPELT
3. CL!MAX
4. ALON E
5. AIR^{SHIP}
6. ^{SUB}MARINE
7. UNCONTROLLABLE GIGGGGGGLLLLLESSSSSSSS
8. DISTANT   FRIENDS

20

How to say 'Hello'

1. You see a friend and say 'Hello!'
2. But a Greek will say 'Rejoice!'
3. A Hebrew will greet you with 'Peace!'
4. The Dutch say 'May you have a hearty dinner!'
5. Germans, like the French, say 'How goes it?'
6. The Poles ask 'Are you happy?'
7. The Chinese enquire, 'Is your stomach in order?'
8. The Moors of history had style when they met you by riding fast at you, pulling up abruptly and firing a gun in the air. That was a greeting worth having.

   Do not take all this as invariable anymore than you invariably say 'Hello'. You might just say 'Hi' or 'How do you do?' So also can the above vary.

Popular misconceptions

1. Pubs and hotels frequently have a room called 'The Buttery' and it is reasonable to suppose the name has something to do with butter. But the word comes from the Middle English word **botery**, which in turn is from the Old French **boteillerie**, a place where bottles are kept.

2. 'Because it is there,' was not a reply by Sir Edmund Hilary to a question about climbing Mount Everest. It was said by George Leigh Mallory, who vanished somewhere on that mountain in 1924.

3. Eve did not eat an apple in the Garden of Eden. There is no reference to it in the Bible. Some say it was an apricot because there are plenty in the Holy Land. The snag about that theory is that apricots are native to China and would have had to travel a long way.

4. The snowdrop is not so named because it is white like a snowflake. The word comes from the German **schneetropfen** meaning a large old-fashioned earring.

5. The chain store is not a modern invention. The first was almost certainly in Japan in the 1600s and started by a brewer of sake in Ise.

6. The late Sir Winston Churchill was not a school dunce. Before he went to Harrow, he was at Stoke Brunswick School in Sussex and records show he was top of the class in all subjects with the exception of geography at which he was second. Churchill himself started the duffer story in his book, 'My Early Life', in which he writes he was unfit for any subject except English.

7. No Christian was ever thrown to the lions or martyred in the Colosseum. It is possible that they suffered indignities at the Circus Maximus (seating about 300,000 compared to the Colosseum's 50,000).

8. The Never-Never Land has nothing to do with Peter Pan. Look again and you will read only of the Neverland.

9. There is no statue of Eros, the God of Love, in or near Piccadilly Circus. That statue is intended to be the Angel of Christian Charity. It was put there in memory of the Earl of Shaftesbury who died in 1885.

10. You cannot escape the consequences of your crime by joining the French Foreign Legion. Contrary to popular belief, the recruiting staff of the Legion vet all volunteers with meticulous care and do not admit criminals.

11. The Great Wall of China is, according to Ripley, the only manmade object visible from the Moon, which is roughly 400,000 kilometres (250,000 miles) away. Astronaut Captain Alan Bean took the trouble to look and writes categorically that even at a distance of only a few thousand miles all that can be seen on the earth is cloud, blue sea, brown desert and patches of green. Nothing manmade can be seen at all.

12. The cross on a hot cross bun is not a Christian symbol, although it is identified with Lent. Hot cross buns were eaten by the ancient Romans, and it has been said that the four quarters of the bun represent the quarters of the Moon.

Unusual collective terms

You are familiar with the collective term for a sheep which is 'flock'. They are not all as easy as that to remember.

For instance:
1. A **muster** of **peacocks**.
2. A **chattering** of **choughs**.
3. A **business** of **ferrets**.
4. A **charm** of **goldfinches**.
5. A **gam** or a **pod** of **whales**.
6. A **watch** of **nightingales**.
7. A **murder** of **crows**.
8. An **exhaltation** of **larks**.
9. A **clamour** of **rooks**.
10. A **skulk** of **foxes**.

<u>The</u> seven wonders of the world

There is more than one list of 7 wonders, but this is the original.

1. **THE PYRAMIDS.** Sometimes all the Egyptian pyramids are included but purists count only the three great pyramids of Khufu, Khafri and Menkaure at Giza.

2. **THE HANGING GARDENS OF BABYLON.** They never hung as their title implies. They were roof gardens. The exact place has never been found, but they were watered from pumps connected to the Euphrates.

3. **THE STATUE OF ZEUS AT OLYMPIA.** This must have been a most wonderful sight as the statue of that god, 9 metres (30 feet) high, was in gold plate seated on a throne also of gold, ivory and possibly gems.

4. **THE TEMPLE OF ARTEMIS AT EPHESUS.** Built around 550 BC, its fame was on two counts: its size, which was over 110 by 55 metres (350 feet by 180 feet), and its display of great works of art.

5. **THE MAUSOLEUM OF HALICARNASSUS.** Halicarnassus is now in Turkey. Mausolus was king of Caria and at his death, c. 350 BC, his widow, Artemisia, built this immense tomb.

6. **THE COLOSSUS OF RHODES.** The bronze-covered statue, internally reinforced with iron, about 30 metres (100 feet) high, was built to the sun-god Helios, so that all whow saw it would remember the raising of the siege of Rhodes in 304 BC. It cost 300 talents, took 12 years to build and was finished in 280 BC.

7. **PHAROS OF ALEXANDRIA.** A lighthouse built on the island of Pharos just off the coast of Alexandria. What the light was is not known for certain — possibly a permanent bonfire at the top or perhaps a mass of oil burners.

Wedding anniversaries
With a few not so well-known ones for good measure.

FIRST	COTTON	TWELFTH	SILK/LINEN
SECOND	PAPER	THIRTEENTH	LACE
THIRD	LEATHER	FOURTEENTH	IVORY
FOURTH	FRUIT/FLOWERS	FIFTEENTH	CRYSTAL
FIFTH	WOODEN	TWENTIETH	CHINA
SIXTH	CHOCS/SWEETS	TWENTY-FIFTH	SILVER
SEVENTH	WOOL/COPPER	THIRTIETH	PEARL
EIGHTH	BRONZE	THIRTY-FIFTH	CORAL
NINTH	POTTERY	FORTIETH	RUBY
TENTH	TIN	FIFTIETH	GOLD
ELEVENTH	STEEL	SIXTIETH	DIAMOND*

*This was confused by Queen Victoria who insisted on her Diamond Jubilee being celebrated after 60 years of her reign.

SEVENTY-FIFTH — if you make it, you get another Diamond Wedding day.

'My ten greatest comedians'
From Bob Monkhouse

1. **BUSTER KEATON** — whose sole concern was getting a laugh with or without words.
2. **HARRY LANGDON** — who knew how to win laughter, but never knew how he knew.
3. **MAX MILLER** — for his mastery of funny vulgarity.
4. **ARTHUR ASKEY** — for never making his audience aware of his detailed comic technique.
5. **BOB HOPE** — for his concealed energy and natural timing.
6. **MAX WALL** — for daring, dedication and a dash of disciplined madness.
7. **W. C. FIELDS** — for cunning effrontery and solid know-how.
8. **PETER SELLERS** — for sharing a sort of genius, a mixture of sheer glee and personal agony, which mingled at its best to produce pure comedy.
9. **GROUCHO MARX** — for being awesome while convulsing the awestruck.
10. **LAUREL AND HARDY** — for never, ever, failing to delight generation after generation.

Ten towns that failed the EEC beach pollution test

TOWN	SEWAGE STATE IN SEA	PEOPLE POLLUTING COAST
1. BLACKPOOL STH SHORE	PART TREATED	213,000
2. EASTBOURNE	PART TREATED	67,000
3. MINEHEAD	RAW & PART TREATED	22,000
4. MORECAMBE	RAW	31,000
5. THE MUMBLES	PART TREATED	128,000
6. PORTHCAWL	RAW	19,000
7. RAMSGATE	PART TREATED	100,000
8. RYDE (I.O.W.)	RAW	5,000
9. SCARBOROUGH S BEACH	RAW	30,000
10. WESTON-S-MARE	PART TREATED	75,000

Since this was issued at mid-summer 1983, the towns may have improved their beaches.

Ten towns that passed the EEC pollution test

1. BOGNOR REGIS
2. BOURNEMOUTH
3. CASWELL BAY
4. HOVE
5. LITTLEHAMPTON
6. NEWQUAY
7. PAIGNTON
8. ST IVES
9. STUDLAND BAY
10. WORTHING

A list of gardens

1. **GARDEN OF EDEN.** This idyllic biblical garden was probably sited in Iraq.
2. **GARDEN OF HESPERIDES.** Hesperides were the three sisters who guarded the golden apples Hera was given as a marriage gift. The garden in which they grew is popularly known as the Garden of Hesperides.
3. **GARDEN OF ENGLAND.** Either Kent or Worcester. Each has that name.
4. **GARDEN OF EUROPE.** Another name for Italy because of its rich vegetation.
5. **GARDEN OF ITALY.** Another name for Sicily.
6. **GARDEN OF THE SUN.** The Malayan Archipelago.
7. **GARDEN OF SWITZERLAND.** Thurgau or Thurgovie, a prosperous agricultural area famed for apples, for cider, and for pears. There are vineyards along the edge of Lake Constance (Bodensee).
8. **GARDEN OF INDIA.** Ayodhya also called Awadh and Oudh. It is one of the seven holy places of the Hindus.
9. **GARDEN OF IRELAND.** This is at Carlow, or in Irish, Ceatharlach, which is on the river Barrow.
10. **GARDEN OF SPAIN.** This is Andalusia which is a historic region in the southernmost part of Spain.

How to address Royalty

You never know when you might be called upon to write to a royal person. If you know the person well it does not matter within reason how you address him or her. But suppose you do not know that person or have met only once. Let us start at the top.

1. **THE QUEEN.**
   On the envelope 'To the Queen's Most Excellent Majesty'.
   Start the letter 'Madam' or 'Your Majesty' or 'May it please Your Majesty'.
   End the letter 'I have the honour to be Your Majesty's most obedient subject and servant.'

2. **THE DUKE OF EDINBURGH.**
   On the evelope 'To His Royal Highness The Duke of Edinburgh'.
   Start the letter 'Sir' or 'Your Royal Highness'.
   End the letter 'I have the honour to be Your Royal Highness's most obedient servant.' (And note Highness's NOT Highness'.)

3. **THE QUEEN MOTHER.**
   On the envelope 'To Her Majesty Queen Elizabeth, the Queen Mother.'
   Start the letter 'Madam' or 'Your Majesty' or 'May it please Your Majesty.'
   End the letter 'I have the honour to be Your Majesty's most obedient servant.'

4. **THE PRINCE OF WALES.**
   On the envelope 'To His Royal Highness, the Prince of Wales'.
   Start the letter 'Sir' or 'Your Royal Highness'.
   End the letter 'I have the honour to be Your Royal Highness's most obedient servant'.

5. **ROYAL PRINCES AND DUKES** should be addressed in the same way as the Duke of Edinburgh.

6. **ROYAL PRINCESSES AND DUCHESSES.**
   On the envelope 'To Her Royal Highness the Princess . . .' or 'To Her Royal Highness the Duchess of . . .'.
   Start the letter 'Madam' or 'Your Royal Highness'.

End the letter 'I have the honour to be Your Royal Highness's most obedient servant.'

7. **DUKES AND DUCHESSES.**
   On the evelope 'To His Grace the Duke of . . .' or 'Her Grace the Duchess of . . .'.
   Start the letter 'Sir' or 'Madam', 'My Lord Duke' or 'Your Grace'. 'Your Grace' will serve both a duke and a duchess. If you know them fairly well, but not intimately, you may start 'Dear Duke' or 'Dear Duchess'.
   End the letter 'I have the honour to be Your Grace's most obedient servant.' Again, depending on how well you know them, you may end 'Yours sincerely.'

Angels in descending order of rank

The commonly used hierarchy of orders is that popularized by the Pseudo-Dionysius order (c. 450 AD) which arranges them in three groups.

The first circle are these three.
1. SERAPHIM.
2. CHERUBIM.
3. THRONES.

These are the second circle.
4. DOMINIONS.
5. VIRTUES.
6. POWERS.

These are the third circle.
7. PRINCIPALITIES.
8. ARCHANGELS.
9. ANGELS.

The seven holy angels are Michael, Gabriel, Raphael, Uriel, Chemuel, Jophiel and Zadkiel.

How to address the Clergy

1. **ARCHBISHOP**
   On the evelope 'To His Grace the Lord Archbishop of . . . .'
   Start the letter 'Dear Lord Archbishop' or 'Your Grace' or
   (proper but rare) 'My Lord Archbishop'.
   End the letter 'Yours sincerely' or 'Yours respectfully' or 'Your
   Lordship's obedient servant.'

2. **BISHOP**
   On the evelope 'To the Right Reverend the Lord Bishop of
   . . . .'
   Start the letter 'Dear Bishop'.
   End the letter 'Yours faithfully' or 'Yours sincerely'. There is an
   old world ending too which is acceptable 'Your most
   obedient servant.'

3. **DEAN**
   On the evelope 'To the Very Reverend Dean of . . .'
   Start the letter 'Dear Dean'.
   End the letter 'Yours sincerely'.

4. **ARCHDEACON**
   On the envelope 'To the Venerable the Archdeacon.'
   Start the letter 'Venerable sir,' or better 'Dear Archdeacon.'
   End the letter 'Yours sincerely,' unless you want to make a
   meal of it but I am assured by an Archdeacon that it will not
   impress him. But if you do, sign your name after 'Your
   obedient servant.'

5. **CANON**
   On the envelope 'The Rev. Canon . . . .' If he is a B.A., an M.A.,
   or a D.D. you must put those initials after his name.
   Start the letter 'Dear Canon . . . .'
   End the letter 'Yours sincerely.'

6. **RABBI**
   On the evelope 'Rabbi . . . .'
   Start the letter 'Dear Rabbi'.
   End the letter 'Yours sincerely'.

Helpful hints on preparing a second hand car for sale

1. Remove all old stickers. If soap and water does not move them, use methylated spirit. Difficult but necessary.
2. Polish the windows and the chrome.
3. Empty the ashtrays.
4. Vacuum the interior.
5. Empty the boot and the glove compartment. Vacuum them thoroughly.
6. Wash the floor mats.
7. Look for and remove foot scuff marks inside the doors where people have pushed open the doors with their shoes.
8. Charge the battery for a day before you try to sell the car. If you can't start it, you can't sell it.
9. Wash it. Wax polish the paint work.
10. Eliminate rattles and vibrations by tightening the offending parts.
11. Check tyres, so that a smooth ride will follow.
12. Produce as much evidence of care (receipts of regular services and other papers) as you can to show a prospective buyer.

A list of colours and what they might mean to those who wear them to excess

(WARNING! Do not take this list too seriously.)

BROWN. Those who wear a lot of brown are quietly assertive and apparently withdrawn. They are thoughtful, careful, kind and considerate, until their own position is threatened. Then they defend their own with complete ruthlessness. Take care not to snub these people: it will cause more distress than is intended. Beware of an excessively secret and basely personal pride.

GREEN. Down through history green has had a reputation for bringing bad luck. It is only lucky for plants. Actions begun by wearers of green to demonstrate their powers of control often end in mishap because of their selfishness. Such people are often self-centred to the exclusion of compassion for others.

MAROON. A colour worn by many people who have two distinct sides to their natures. One side is passionate, enjoying good food and drink and is sociable. The other side is capable of great restraint, aesthetic perception and appreciation of the arts. Sometimes the one will break across the boundary of the other, especially with music and the arts where sensuous artistry will dominate finer feelings.

ORANGE. The wearer of orange likes to stand out in a crowd. There is nothing subtle about this wearer. The colour says 'Here I am! I am what I am and you can like me or not. That's not my worry.' He or she refuses to accept set ideas without examining them first in detail. Is a completely loyal friend.

RED. This shows a warm impulsive personality. He or she is sexy, outgoing, creative and likes it to be known; probably talks a little too much; is not very good at keeping secrets; likes to be liked and is afraid of loneliness. Enjoys friendship and close personal relationships; does not tolerate fools and can be depended upon to keep promises. This is because of a strong streak of over-conscientiousness.

BLACK. People who dress in this are strong-minded, frequently wrong and liberal with their misguided views. People who wear black because they like it (rather than to disguise their overweight proportions) do not make friends easily, and having made friends will lose them or change them frequently because of being so outspoken.

YELLOW. A man or woman who wears this to excess will be most direct in all dealings, both with friends and in business. Will always come straight to the point whether dealing with romance or selling nuts and bolts. You will enjoy any relationship with such a person, because you will always know where you are. There will be no deceits and no compromises.

WHITE AND CREAM. People, almost always women, who wear this (other than on sporting occasions which demand white or cream) are fastidious, careful, house-proud and introspective. Do not like clutter in or around the house and bric-a-brac is something beyond their comprehension, because they are often artistic and demand simplicity in all things.

BLUE. Those who wear blue are thoughtful, introspective and careful. If success comes to such a person, it is because of sheer persistence and planning. Will seldom, if ever, be impulsive or do something that has not been thought out thoroughly in advance. Perhaps there is an overcaring attitude to what others think of them.

VIOLET AND PURPLE. These show an inability to come to terms with realism. Will thoroughly enjoy such doubtful happenings as flying saucers, the Loch Ness Monster or the occult in all its many shades. Some psychiatrists say that people with such beliefs have never quite grown up, and should, for instance the Loch Ness Monster one day be proved to exist and put on exhibition, wearers of violet would be disappointed.

Frequent misquotations

Beneath each one will be found the correct version.

1. Home is the sailor, home from the sea.
   (**Home is the sailor, home from sea.** R. L. Stevenson)
2. To gild refined gold, to gild the lily.
   (**To gild refined gold, to paint the lily.** Shakespeare)
3. Fresh fields and pastures new.
   (**Fresh woods and pastures new.** Milton)
4. I am escaped by the skin of my teeth.
   (**I am escaped with the skin of my teeth.** Bible)
5. Oh to be in England, now that April's here.
   (**Oh to be in England, now that April's there.** Browning)
6. Elementary! My dear Watson.
   (**'Excellent!' I (Dr Watson) cried. 'Elementary!' said he**
   (Holmes).
   Nowhere in any Conan Doyle work does the phrase
   'Elementary! My dear Watson!' appear.)
7. The shrinking violet thus did I chide!
   (**The forward violet thus did I chide!** Shakespeare)
8. Music hath charms to sooth a savage beast.
   (**Music has charms to sooth a savage breast.** Congreve)
9. You dirty rat! (James Cagney)
   (**Cagney never once said this in any film.**)
10. The Battle of Waterloo was won on the playing fields of Eton.
    (Duke of Wellington).
    He never said it. When Wellington was at Eton there were no
    playing fields.

A booze news list
The four greatest beer producing countries.
(1983 figures)

1.	**USA**	138,900,000 barrels
2.	**WEST GERMANY**	57,300,000 barrels
3.	**USSR**	38,400,000 barrels
4.	**UK**	37,700,000 barrels

(Figures from the Brewers' Society.)

Unsolicited mail found on my hall mat

The following is a description of the contents of mail privately delivered over the course of one month. How does it compare with the rubbish you get?

1. An invitation (at a price) to a concert performed by an unknown ensemble with an unknown conductor and featuring unknown soloists.
2. An invitation to 'have a new bedroom with nothing to pay — for six months'.
3. An offer of a ski service with 10 per cent off anything I might want to buy there on condition I bring the leaflet.
4. An announcement of the opening of a new restaurant (or it could be an old one wanting new custom, there is no way of finding out) which is nowhere near where I live. The write-up leaves out the main sales points: no menu, no prices and no mention of parking facilities.
5. A car service which will take me anywhere reliably and courteously. Again the main sales point has been left out: no prices for distances.
6. A very expensive window cleaning service.
7. A highly suspect piece of advertising with a hidden number. On rubbing the surface from that number I find I am a prize winner — but the prize, priced at £9.99 looks worth about £1.50 — but it *is* a prize and I have won. I look again and see I am asked for £2.00 postage and packing.
8. I am asked to join a slimming club. Not a bad idea but I do not have a weight problem.
9. 'Enrol now!' The piece of paper says that if I am over 14 I should learn typing, shorthand and book keeping. This is the most reasonable offer yet, though there is still no mention of cost.
10. Now I find an instruction not to sell or buy a house without consulting a local estate agent. He is probably excellent but I am not thinking of selling.
11. Immediately under it and arriving at the same time is a message from another estate agent telling me I should let my house. With it is a list of rich firms, mostly foreign, who need to rent property for their staff.
12. Now I am told I can be 'bronzed and beautiful with our very special offer of 6 highspeed sunbed sessions for £30'

provided I bring the voucher. I telephoned the number on the voucher, lied, and said I had lost the bit of paper which was a condition of getting the 'very special offer'. Yes, you guessed it. I would be welcome with or without the voucher and could still have the 'very special offer'.

13. I am asked again and still no price mentioned, by a different school, to learn typing and so on. Why are these people so shy of putting in the price?

14. I find a piece of paper that at first looks like an offer to clean all my carpets for nothing, but on closer inspection the offer actually applies to something (it does not say if it is a book, a booklet, or even a pamphlet) FREE which tells you how to take care of your carpets. In other words it is a genuine FREE offer – *after* you have become a customer.

15. I find a fascinating offer by a large company telling me how I can increase my capital – if I pass it to them first.

16. This did not come through the post but it has a phoney Cornish post mark. It is a postcard telling me 'Just to let you know we discovered Gold Top Butter is made in Cornwall . . .' As it is signed Gold Top it seems odd that they appear to have only just discovered where they make the stuff.

17. I have an offer to be made beautiful at home. The offer

suggests I discuss my beauty problems with the lady who signs the advertisement and advocates, among other treatments, 'waxing'. I immediately thought of the car. I wonder what she would charge for doing it.

18. Another warning not to sell my house without first talking to another estate agent.
19. An offer to be given (sold would be a better word) driving lessons.
20. Five hire car cards all at once from the same firm, which, like the previous hire car firm forgets to put the price per mile.
21. I have an offer from a Japanese letting agency to fill my house with 'A — CLASS' Japanese.
22. Somebody again offers to make me look beautiful. These beauty ads do not include a money back guarantee — should they fail to make me beautiful. Perhaps they caught a glimpse of me through the letter box first.

Bob Monkhouse lists 'My ten worst puns'

1. Racial superiority is a pigment of your imagination.
2. The man who wrote 'God Save The Queen' must have been an anthem devil.
3. The baker who sliced four loaves of bread at once with a meat axe was known as a 4-loaf cleaver.
4. My elm tree is peeling badly, but is recovering from Dutch Elm Disease. Its bark is worse than its blight.
5. I got so drunk one night I didn't know which side my broad was better on.
6. There's a branch of science devoted to the study of corns among dogs with hard paws. It's called 'Hard Paw Cornography'.
7. I threw a bucket of *Brobat* over a Roman Catholic father and got arrested for bleach of the priest.
8. You can't always detect your own vanity, but others conceit.
9. There was a fire at the detergent factory. The walls fell in with a thickening sud.
10. Asked to make a pun about the Japanese I begged, 'Give a Japan-easy one.' But to pun about an Israeli — Israeli impossible.
P.S. Do ghost trains stop at manifest stations?

100 people were asked 'What do you want out of life above all else?'

This was how they answered.

41% said	**GOOD HEALTH**
27% said	**MONEY**
11% said	**HAPPINESS**
8% said	**PEACE**
7% said	**TRAVEL**
6% said	**LOVE**

No one wanted more brains. Rather a shame really.

Squid facts

1. The squids seen in underwater horror films are imaginary animals only.
2. Squids are feeble and even if one should make a sluggish grab at you, it can be shaken off with ease.
3. Very few of them attain any size. A squid of the deep can be 21 metres (65 feet) long and weigh half a ton but it is unlikely to come anywhere near the surface except by mistake.
4. Large squid can be active only in the intense cold of the deeps. Warm surface water seems to drain the big ones of most energy.
5. In relation to its size, its eight tentacles are short compared to those of an octopus.
6. In addition to the eight short tentacles it has two long ones for catching its prey.
7. A full grown squid can be less than 1.5 cm (¾ inch) long.
8. Some young resemble the adult. Some go through a larval stage.
9. Some are luminous to attract prey.
10. They are eaten by bony fish, man and especially the sperm whale.

Main causes of road accidents

Compiled for this book by Alex Greene of the R.A.C. in his capacity of Highways, Traffic and Road Safety Engineer.

1. Lack of anticipation.
2. Driving too close to the vehicle in front.
3. Poor signalling.
4. Poor observation.
5. Overtaking without proper care.
6. Turning right without proper care and **positioning**.
7. Pedestrians not following kerb drill.
8. Inadequate use of rear view mirror.
9. Lack of consideration for other road users, too much aggression.
10. Not taking due care in adverse road or weather conditions.
11. Failure to use lights in poor visibility.
12. Cyclists riding without lights.
13. Driving with dirty or frosted-up windscreens.
14. Poor street lighting.
15. Inadequate warning signs particularly at roadworks.
16. Poor road layout.
17. Poor road markings, particularly signs and road markings.

Fictitious detectives

DETECTIVE	CREATOR
1. Arsène Lupin	Maurice Leblanc
2. Bulldog Drummond	Herman Cyril McNeil (Sapper)
3. Charlie Chan	Earl Derr Biggers
4. Hercule Poirot	Agatha Christie
5. Inspector Maigret	Georges Simenon
6. James Bond	Ian Fleming
7. Jane Marple	Agatha Christie
8. Perry Mason	Erle Stanley Gardner
9. Lord Peter Wimsey	Dorothy L. Sayers
10. Philip Marlowe	Raymond Chandler
11. Sherlock Holmes	Arthur Conan Doyle
12. Sergeant Cuff	Wilkie Collins
13. Simon Templar (The Saint)	Leslie Charteris
14. Inspector Javert	Victor Hugo

Names that have been or are still registered trade names

1. ESCALATOR
2. GRAMOPHONE
3. ASPIRIN
4. YO-YO
5. FIBREGLASS
6. UNDERSEAL
7. MILK OF MAGNESIA
8. PETROL
9. COKE
10. CORNFLAKES
11. LIBERTY BODICE

(Petrol was originally sold under the name of Motor Spirit until the name Petrol was registered. If you order a Coke you should be served ONLY Coca Cola. Any other Cola is not Coke.)

Alcohol proof systems

If you have a bottle (most unlikely) which is one hundred percent alcohol, the US label will read 200 proof, the UK label will read 175 proof and that is downright confusing. So now take a look at the following:

1. **51.7%** pure alcohol	US **114.3** proof	UK **100** proof
2. **50%** pure alcohol	US **100** proof	UK **87.5** proof
3. **42.9%** pure alcohol	US **85.7** proof	UK **75** proof
4. **37.1%** pure alcohol	US **74.3** proof	UK **65** proof
5. **30%** pure alcohol	US **60** proof	UK **52.5** proof
6. **20%** pure alcohol	US **40** proof	UK **35** proof
7. **10%** pure alcohol	US **20** proof	UK **17.5** proof

It is still not clear why the manufacturers of gin, vodka and whisky and other alcohol drinks cannot just put on the bottle something simple like 'contains 30% pure alcohol'.

British born inventors

1. **WILLIAM LEE: the first knitting machine in 1589.** He was a clergyman, born in Calverton, Nottinghamshire, who persisted in perfecting his idea, because the woman he was courting was more interested in knitting than in him.

2. **JOHN NAPIER** (sometimes spelled Neper): **invented logarithms in 1614.** He was born at Merchiston Castle near Edinburgh. His invention sprang from comparing arithmetic and geometric progressions (see also page 182).

3. **WILLIAM GASCOIGNE: the micrometer in 1636.** It is mainly used for measuring within $\frac{1}{1000}$th of an inch and less.

4. **THOMAS SAVERY: the steam pump in 1638.** It worked by atmospheric pressure pushing a cylinder down after it had been raised by steam. The steam was condensed quickly by the application of cold water.

5. **JOHN HARRISON: the chronometer** (an accurate and portable time piece) **in 1735.** This was as a result of a Government competition. The aim was to cut shipping losses. The reward £20,000. Harrison won, proved by a voyage from England to Jamaica in 1761. He was only 1¼ miles off course after 6 weeks at sea. When he claimed his reward, it was dealt out to him in pennies in odd instalments. He did not receive the full amount until three years before his death in 1776.

6. **THOMAS SAINT: the sewing machine in 1790.** Many people claim to have fathered it but his principle established it. He took out the first patent for a machine to stitch shoes. It was not successful until many others had made improvements, notably the American Elias Howe who, after a dream of being wounded by wild men whose spears had holes in the sharp end, suddenly thought of putting the hole at the tip of the needle rather than in the middle as Saint had done.

7. **DAVID BREWSTER: the kaleidoscope in 1817.** The original purpose of this was to help textile designers. It later became a children's toy.

8. **CHARLES BABBAGE: the automatic computer.** This mathematician and inventor, made 1823 a most important year: later developments of his invention have since swept the world (see also page 183).

9. **JOHN WALKER: the first modern match in 1827.** (They were known in another form in markets of Hanchow (China) in A.D. 970.)

10. **SIR FRANK WHITTLE: the jet engine in 1930.** The first flight with such an engine was on May 15, 1941 fitted to a Gloster E28/39 frame.

Travellers' last minute panics

During a long wait at London (Heathrow) Airport I produced a list of things that potential travellers might have forgotten. There is always so much hanging about at airports that while I created a minor panic — you will see why — people were delighted by the diversion of being asked to tick off what they might have forgotten. I presented the list in alphabetical order and have since rearranged it in numerical order.

DID YOU FORGET	THOSE WHO HAD TO THINK TWICE (%)
TO LOCK UP HOUSE?	25
TRAVELLERS' CHEQUES/MONEY?	19
PASSPORT?	18
TO TURN OFF WATER AT HOME?	15
TO STOP THE PAPERS?	8
TO TURN OFF THE GAS?	6
TO TURN OFF ELECTRICITY?	5
SLEEPING OR OTHER PILLS?	2
THESE FORGOT NOTHING (or said so)	2

Quite a few rather more suspicious people thought I was some sort of Government snoop and told me to mind my own business. One man, slightly inebriated, told his wife to ignore me as I must be a burglar.

A list of futilities

None of this information will do you the slightest good.

1. In Italy you can buy a rotating crucifix with a gaudy Christ on it wobbling round and round to a grating version of 'Come Back to Sorrento.'
2. Wild animals do not snore.
3. If a Tibetan passes a woman in the street, he sticks his tongue out at her and she likes it. It is a good-mannered greeting.
4. Never send a Chinese woman in China a picture of a stork, if she has just had a baby, because the stork there is a symbol of death.
5. Never emphasize a point by thumping the table in front of a Malaysian. He will think this so rude he may walk out of the room.
6. Cock and Bull stories take their name from two inns at Stoney Stratford, Bucks. They were coaching inns in the early 1700s where travellers from the north would meet those from the south and exchange their travellers' tales. Hence Cock and Bull stories.
7. The late Gerald Du Maurier, an actor of note, once sent this cryptic message '8 COME 9'. The recipient took a long time to work it out as 'Come between eight and nine'. So long did he take, he missed the meeting.
8. The Romans, as will be found elsewhere in this book, cooked and ate dormice stuffed with a variety of flavours from minced pork to honey. What is not generally known is that their dormouse snobbery was equivalent to our wine snobbery.
9. French medieval King, Philip Augustus, decreed that the longer the points on his subjects' shoes the higher the rank.
10. The longest title of any piece of published music is 'Green with Envy, Purple with Passion, White with Anger, Scarlet with Fever, What Were You Doing in Her Arms Last Night Blues.' It was written by Phillip Springer and Nita Jones in 1961.
11. The board game Monopoly is outlawed in the USSR.
12. If he is not bald, the average man has about 5,000,000 hairs growing simultaneously.

Ten frequently told lies

1. Sorry to be late. Fred was kept at the office.
2. What a beautiful baby!
3. You can tell **me**. I'll never repeat it to anyone.
4. No, we don't have a microwave oven (or washing machine, spin dryer, dishwasher etc.) because they just don't do the job properly.
5. Where did you get that frock (tie, shirt etc.)? I think it's gorgeous.
6. We have to have this little car because a bigger one won't fit the garage.
7. Thank you very much for (the present)! It's just what I wanted.
8. Of course we wrote! It must have been lost in the post.
9. No, I never bother to read my horoscope.
10. Someone must have run into the car while I was in a shop.

A list of clichés

My own, no doubt biased, definition of a cliché is a phrase that is used too often and is an unnecessary substitute for plain English.

1. Keeping a low profile.
2. Having said that.
3. In point of fact.
4. Up for grabs.
5. At the end of the day.
6. The money on the table. (Often linked to 5.)
7. A meaningful dialogue.
8. At this point in time. (Sometimes varied to 'At this moment in time' which is tautology as all **moments** are **time**.)
9. Run out of steam.
10. No way. (When not used literally. For example: 'Will you be going to Blackpool this year?' 'No way!')

11. We explored every avenue.
12. It's a rip-off!
13. An on-going situation.
14. A feed-back from the grass roots.
15. You know as well as I do.

16. Let's put it this way. (Only excusable when used by removal men trying to get a grand piano through the door.)
17. Ethnic minorities.
18. Spend money as if there was no tomorrow.
19. Not to be sneezed at.
20. Free collective bargaining.

The ten most used words in this book

or so my word processor tells me.

1. THE
2. A
3. OF
4. AND
5. TO
6. IN
7. IS
8. YOU
9. THAT
10. IT

Animals in Chinese years

The year of the **HARE** or **RABBIT**	1975
The year of the **DRAGON**	1976
The year of the **SNAKE** or **SERPENT**	1977
The year of the **HORSE**	1978
The year of the **SHEEP** or **GOAT**	1979
The year of the **MONKEY**	1980
The year of the **COCK**	1981
The year of the **DOG**	1982
The year of the **PIG** or **BOAR**	1983
The year of the **RAT**	1984
The year of the **OX**	1985
The year of the **TIGER**	1986

Famous remarks

1. 'I read War and Peace in ten minutes; it's about Russia.'
   Woody Allen
2. 'Nostalgia isn't what it used to be.' **Peter de Vries**
3. 'Never believe anything until it's been officially denied.'
   Katherine Whitehorn
4. 'I would not talk so much about myself if there were
   anybody else whom I knew as well.' **Henry D. Thoreau**
5. 'Trifles make perfection and perfection is no trifle.'
   Michelangelo

6. 'Strip away the phoney tinsel of Hollywood and you find the
   real tinsel underneath.' **Oscar Levant**
7. 'Too caustic? To hell with the cost; we'll make the picture
   anyway.' **Sam Goldwyn**
8. 'Marriage is the only adventure open to the cowardly.'
   Voltaire
9. 'The money is a life belt thrown to a swimmer who has
   already reached the shore in safety.' **George Bernard Shaw**
   (of the Nobel Prize)
10. 'Democracy is the worst form of government — except all
    those other forms that have been tried from time to time.'
    Winston Churchill

11. 'No man is a hero to his own wife; no woman is a wife to her own hero.' **No one knows who said this.**
12. 'Man is the cleverest of animals, and the most stupid.' **Diogenes**
13. 'He had the sort of face that once seen is never remembered.' **Oscar Wilde**
14. 'Keep Christmas white.' **Charles Chilton** (to Spike Milligan)
15. 'We must believe in luck. For how else can we explain the success of those we don't like?' **Cocteau**
16. 'Our telephone answering device is being repaired, this is a person speaking.' **Eric Burgin**

A list from astronomer Patrick Moore

Asked to write a list of astonishing facts about our universe, he sent me this.

1. **LIFE.** Because the origin of life involves so many improbable features. I realize that we have no proof of life beyond Earth, but the Earth is, after all, in space, so I think we qualify.
2. **QUASARS** – because of their incredible energy output.
3. **NEUTRON STARS** (pulsars) because of their incredible density.
4. **THE CRAB NEBULA,** because it emits so strongly over such a wide range of the electromagnetic spectrum.
5. **SATURN'S RINGS,** because of their amazing complexity.
6. **THE 3° BACKGROUND RADIATION** coming in in all directions, because it may be a remnant of the Big Bang of c. 15,000,000,000 years ago.
7. **EPSILON AURIGAE,** which is a weird system made up of a very luminous supergiant plus a companion which is huge but transparent – we wouldn't know of its existence but for the fact that every 27 years it passes in front of the supergiant and dims it by a magnitude.
8. **ALBIREO** (Beta Cygni), a lovely coloured double star with a golden yellow primary and gloriously blue companion.
9. **ETA CARINAE,** the extraordinary southern star which rose to its peak in the 1840s, when it was as powerful as around 6,000,000 Suns – and is still amazing even though it has faded (perhaps because its radiations are partly blocked by interstellar matter.)

A list about Patrick Moore

1. He was born in 1923.
2. His interest in astronomy began early. He joined the British Astronomical Association in 1934 and is the current President.
3. His main researches have been in connection with the moon and the planets.
4. He plays the xylophone. (Royal Command Performance in 1981!)
5. He has his own private observatory at his home in Selsey.
6. Among his likes are breakfast and good wine, though not together.
7. He dislikes beetroot.

Cocktails from three masters of the art

These exotic drinks have been selected by three outstanding exponents of the art of mixing a stunning cocktail. The first five are from A. R. Fairlie, one of the directors of the 'Howtowdie' restaurant in Edinburgh.

1. Howtowdie Special. Mix Van Der Hum with whisky, Grenadine, egg white and orange juice. How much of each? Never mind — keep trying until you get it right.*
2. Mata Hari. Dry gin with Triple Sec, Pisang and lemon juice.
3. Once Is Enough. Bacardi with Banane, Galliano and orange. (Try orange juice or just a slice of orange.)
4. Jungle Juice. Pisang with Apricot brandy, gin, lemon juice and orange.
5. Blue Surfer. Kontiki with Blue Curaçao, dry gin and crushed ice.

Moving south, the next five come from Bob Burton, Head Bartender of the famous Ritz restaurant in London — a man of immense experience at making perfect drinks.

6. Vodka or Gin Ricky. Take an old-fashioned glass, add the juice of 1 lime, a measure of spirit poured over the ice and a dash of soda.
7. Felicity's Downfall. Take an old-fashioned glass, add crushed ice, 3/10 Malibu, 1/5 Campari and 1/2 grapefruit juice.

8. Pink Velvet. Take a champagne glass, mix Dubonnet, Cointreau, grapefruit juice, a dash of egg white and top it up with Ritz Rosé. The quantities were not revealed – obviously one of Bob Burton's secrets.
9. Sours. You have to experiment a little* to find out which one of these you like best. Take a cocktail glass, add a bar-spoon or sugar, the juice of 1 lemon, a dash of Angostura, and after that you can mix in any of these – whisky, brandy or any one of the many liqueurs available.
10. Perfect Manhattan. Straight up or on the rocks. Take a cocktail glass, add a dash of Angostura, 1/6 sweet red Martini, 1/6 dry Martini, 2/3 rye whiskey and decorate the glass with a cherry and a twist of lemon.

Finally five from Tony Fray, Head Bartender of the Berkeley. He is the winner of many UK and international prizes for his creations. The list begins with one created specially for this book.

11. Octopus. 2/6 brandy, 2/6 Peach nectar, 1/6 Fraise de Bois, 1/6 lemon juice and a dash of Benedictine. Add a little champagne or sparkling white wine. Serve in a large cocktail glass.

12. Renaissance. ⅖ vodka, ⅖ orange juice, ⅕ Mandarin Napoleon and some tonic water. Blend, then pour into a 15 oz pina colada glass with ice. Decorate with orange, cherry, umbrella and straws.
13. Spring Fever. ⅓ Apricot brandy, ⅓ Bacardi rum, ⅓ Coconut cream and a dash of double cream. Blend, then serve in a 15 oz pina colada glass with ice. Sprinkle nutmeg on top.
14. Special Berkeley Cooler. ½ brandy, ¼ orange juice, ¼ lemon juice and 3 dashes of Apricot brandy. Blend, then serve in a 15 oz pina colada glass with ice. Top up with sparkling wine or champagne. Decorate with a slice of orange and straws.
15. Electric Summer. ½ vodka, ¼ Mandarin Napoleon, ¼ lemon juice, 3 dashes of Blue Curaçao and white of egg. Blend, then serve in a large cocktail glass. Decorate with a cherry.

Tony Fray adds this note of interest to all who stand on the customer's side of the bar. 'Any cocktail that wins a National Cocktail Competition is automatically registered by the United Kingdom Bartenders' Guild.'

*Experience tells me not to try too many experiments all on the same evening.

Events during the building of Nelson's column in Trafalgar Square

1. Sir Edwin Landseer, the sculptor of the lions, was almost always drunk. (He worked on the lions from 1859-66.)
2. The people stoned the lions when they were first displayed.
3. The workmen were idle and also drunk.
4. Because of 1 and 3, the work took 30 years.
5. This resulted in protest meetings in the square.
6. The statue of Nelson, weighing 18 tons, had to be hauled up twice because sloppy workmanship at first showed the crane to be 14 feet (4 metres) too short.
7. The crane was not 14 feet (4 metres) too short. Sloppy workmanship had caused the column to be 14 feet (4 metres) too tall. It still is.

A list about Angela Willans

1. She has been editor of the Problems Page in *Woman's Own* for the past 20 years.
2. She used to write under the pseudonym Mary Grant.
3. She is a graduate of London University.
4. She has been a teacher . . .
5. . . . a tutor for handicapped children;
6. . . . a shop assistant;
7. . . . a canteen waitress.
8. She's on the executive of the National Marriage Guidance Council.
9. She's a council member of One-Parent Families, Brook Advisory Centres and the British Humanist Association.
10. Her postbag averages 400 letters a week.

Ten most frequent problems from Angela Willans

Here are the subjects of her ten most frequent problems.

1. **LONELINESS** — from the friendless and unattached.
2. **LONELINESS** — from people who *feel* isolated, though having friends.
3. **LONELINESS** — from people in relationships who cannot communicate.
4. **LONELINESS** — from people whose relationships have broken down e.g. divorced, bereaved, rejected.
5. **LONELINESS** — the circumstantial kind e.g. moved to new area, tied to home with a baby and husband works away.
6. **LACK OF CONFIDENCE**, insecurity, 'pardon me for living'.
7. **MARRIAGE AND COHABITATION PROBLEMS** — number one is infidelity.
8. **SEX.**
9. **STRESS.**
10. **FAMILY** — single parents, step-children, adolescent worries, in-laws, violence, divorce and separation etc.

Memorable occasions in the history of flight

1. **1783: LIFT OFF.** On June 5, 1783, Joseph and Etienne Montgolfier launched a spherical balloon of paper and linen, which was about 9 metres (30 feet) in diameter. It was open at the bottom, so that heat from a fire could be collected inside. It stayed aloft for about ten minutes, during which time it rose to 2,000 metres (6,000 feet).

2. **1853: WINGS AWAY.** Sir George Cayley, a Yorkshireman, became the now acknowledged inventor of the aeroplane. In 1853 he launched an improved version of a pervious triplane, which carried his coachman across a valley near Brompton, Yorkshire. The trip was uneventful but the world's first passenger in a heavier-than-air machine left shortly afterwards to get another job.

3. **1903: POWER TO THE PEOPLE.** Wilbur and Orville Wright designed and flew the first *powered* heavier-than-air machine. This first flight was over a distance of 37 metres.

4. **1909: UP, ROUND AND DOWN.** Igor Sikorsky, a Russian, designed and built the first large helicopter. The drawback was that, while it could lift itself from the ground, it didn't have enough power left to take a pilot.

5. **1919: USA NON-STOP.** Two Englishmen, Captain John Alcock and Lt Arthur Brown were the first to cross the Atlantic in a powered aeroplane (a Vickers Vimy) flying non-stop.)

6. **1929: ROUND THE WORLD.** This was the year of the first round-the-world flight by an airship. It was developed by the Germans.

7. **1939: UP, ROUND AND OFF.** Igor Sikorsky (see 1909) made his first successful flight in a single rotor helicopter.

8. **1944: BOMBS AWAY.** The first V.1. missile, also called the Buzz Bomb and the Flying Bomb, was launched by the Germans and it landed in England. It had a range of 240 km (150 miles).

9. **1952: ALL ABOARD.** The world's first jet airliner, the British-made Comet, went into passenger service from London to Johannesburg.

10. **1968: FASTER THAN SOUND.** Russia's Tu 144, the first super-sonic passenger airliner, had its maiden flight. On June 3, 1973, a Tu 144 exploded in mid-air near Goussainville, France.

The eight major religions
In numerical order of adherents.

1. **CHRISTIANS.** There are roughly 1,000,000,000 Christians in the world of which just over half are Roman Catholics, about 330,000,000 are Protestants, 95,000,000 Eastern Orthodox and the rest a multiplicity which include Jehovah's Witnesses, Gnostics, Congregationalists, Calvinists, Quakers, 7th Day Adventists and numerous other sects and divisions.

2. **MUSLIMS.** There are about 500,000,000 Muslims. The Holy Book of the Muslims is the Koran.

3. **HINDUS.** At least 400,000,000 people are Hindus. Benares is the holiest city. The Ganges is the holiest river.

4. **CONFUCIANS.** There are about 300,000,000 followers of Confucius the Chinese wise man.

5. **BUDDHISTS.** There are about 200,000,000 Buddhists.

6. **SHINTO.** This is the national faith of Japan. About 50,000,000 out of the total population of Japan (100,000,000) are Shintoists.

7. **TAOISM.** Tao is a religion of China with some 30,000,000 adherents out of the total Chinese population of about 900,000,000. The Holy Book of Taoism is called Tao Te Ching.

8. **JUDAISM.** A word encompassing the religious beliefs including the observances of the Jews. About 15,000,000 are adherents to a greater or lesser degree.

A list of boxers from Henry Cooper OBE, KSG

He writes 'This is my list of ten of the greatest fighters, I think they all would have made it no matter what era they had boxed in.'
FIRST THE OLD SCHOOL:

BOXER	LIVED	CHAMPION YEARS
JACK JOHNSON	1878-1946	**Heavyweight** 26.12.08 to 05.04.15.
JACK DEMPSEY	1895-1983	**Heavyweight** 04.07.19 to 23.09.26.
JOE LOUIS	1914-81	**Heavyweight** 22.06.37 to 25.06.48.
HENRY ARMSTRONG	1912-	**Featherweight** 29.10.37 relinquished. **Lightweight** 17.08.38 to 22.08.38. **Welterweight** 31.05.38 to 04.10.40.
TED KID LEWIS	1894-1970	**Welterweight** 01.08.15 to 24.04.16. **Welterweight** 25.06.17 to 17.03.19.

... NOW THE MODERN:

BOXER	LIVED	CHAMPION YEARS
SUGAR RAY ROBINSON	1920-	**Welterweight** 20.12.46 relinquished. **Middleweight** 14.02.51 to 10.07.51. **Middleweight** 12.09.51 relinquished. **Middleweight** 19.12.55 to 02.01.57. **Middleweight** 01.05.57 to 23.09.57. **Middleweight** 25.03.58 to 22.01.60.
ROCKY MARCIANO	1923-69	**Heavyweight** 23.09.52 to 1955 retired.

MUHAMMED ALI	1942-	**Heavyweight** 25.02.64 to 28.04.67 stripped.
		Heavyweight 30.10.74 to 15.02.78.
		Heavyweight 15.09.78 relinquished 1979.
SUGAR RAY LEONARD	1956-	**Welterweight** 30.11.79 to 20.06.80.
		Welterweight 26.11.80 relinquished
ARCHIE MOORE	1916-	**Light heavyweight** 23.09.52 to 1955 retired.

My thanks also to R. L. Clarke O.B.E. of the British Boxing Board of Control for supplying dates and weights.

Nine references to a gentleman

1. He who talks of being a gentleman, can never be one. (Robert Smith Surtees)
2. The word is best used on the door of the men's washroom.
3. From the Old French *gentilz hom*. A man entitled to bear arms but he is not of the nobility.
4. A mole. *The gentleman in black velvet.* The Jacobites drank to the mole that formed the molehill which tripped William III's horse and killed the king.
5. The old gentleman. A playing card slightly longer, wider or in other ways different, but not noticeably so, from the rest of the pack. It's used for identification by card sharps.
6. A gentleman is he who uses the butter knife when on his own.
7. A gentleman is one who never hurts anyone's feelings unintentionally. (Oliver Herford)
8. If a man is a gentleman, he knows quite enough, and if he is not a gentleman, whatever he knows is bad for him. (Oscar Wilde)
9. Manners and money make a gentleman. (Thomas Fuller)
10. You can do business with anyone, but you can only sail a boat with a gentleman. (J. P. Morgan Snr)

Downstairs and upstairs with Margaret Powell

The much loved broadcaster and writer, who sadly died in April 1984, had sent me this list of eight 'emotions' earlier in the year.

1. **CONSTERNATION** on finding, in my first place as a kitchenmaid, that I had to set a box-trap to catch the cockroaches and then tip them — alive — into the fire.
2. **HUMILIATION,** also as a kitchenmaid, on being severely reprimanded for handing the morning newspapers to Madam — instead of first placing them on the salver.
3. **STUPEFACTION** at not only having to polish the INSTEPS of the boots and shoes — which we never did at home — but having to take out Madam's shoe-laces every morning and iron them.
4. **AGITATION** when, as Cook to an Italian lady — who always worked out the menu with me while she was in the bath — I entered one morning to find, not Madam, but a nude man standing in the bath. Hastily departing, face fiery red — girls were unsophisticated in those days — I was consoled by the butler saying 'Don't upset yourself, Cook, it was probably only a loofah!'
5. **DELECTATION** when the aforesaid butler made me one of his special cocktails, which he did every time he asked me to marry him. His favourite saying was 'All a man wants in life is comfort and love.' He thought Madam could supply the comfort and me the love.
6. **MORTIFICATION** when being expected to sing on a television programme and practising for two hours with three musicians, the session ended wtih the words 'I think, Mrs Powell, it would be better if we followed you.'
7. **GRATIFICATION** and gloom of constant fan-mail. Some all sweetness and light; 'loved your books, laughed all the time!' Others; 'my two-year-old could write better than you, read the first six pages, that was enough!'
8. **IMAGINATION**, after years of only just surviving; what shall I do with the money, how to spend it? Found no difficulty at all. Was reproached on a radio programme for saying this. Was told 'I thought you believed in the equal distribution of wealth.' Replied 'Ah, that was before I got any!'

100 people asked to name a bad luck superstition they *believed* in said this:

(We did not have any 'don't knows' or 'not superstitious' because when we met some, and there were several, we left them out and went on to find the superstitious.)

23 said **Never** walk under a ladder.
21 said **Don't** let a black cat cross your path.
14 said A **broken mirror** means seven years' bad luck.
11 said **Never** use the number thirteen.
10 said **Crossed knives** mean a quarrel.
 9 said An **inverted horseshoe** lets your good luck run out.
 8 said Seeing one **magpie** brings bad luck.
 4 said It is **unlucky** to pass someone on the stairs unless you cross your fingers.

(Note. Those who said they were superstitious but could not think of anything were shown the above list.)

Names which have changed

OLD NAME	NOW CALLED
1. Batavia	Djakarta
2. Belgian Congo	Zaire
3. Ceylon	Sri Lanka
4. Christiania	Oslo
5. Ciudad Trujillo	Santo Domingo
6. Constantinople	Istanbul
7. Danzig	Gdansk
8. East Pakistan	Bangladesh
9. Gold Coast	Ghana
10. Mesopotamia	Iraq
11. Northern Rhodesia	Zambia
12. Peiping	Peking
13. Persia	Iran
14. St Petersburg	Leningrad
15. Siam	Thailand
16. Stalingrad	Volvograd
17. Tanganyika	Tanzania

Ten common tautological expressions

The Oxford Dictionary defines 'tautology' as a repetition of the same word or phrase, or of the same idea or statement in other words. It adds that it is usually 'as a fault of style'.

1. **FREE GIFT**
2. **ADEQUATE ENOUGH**
3. **FINAL COMPLETION**
4. **FINAL UPSHOT**
5. **JUST EXACTLY**
6. **FUNERAL OBSEQUIES**
7. **TWO TWINS**
8. **UNCOMMONLY STRANGE**
9. **YOUNG INFANT**
10. This book is **NOT LIMITED ONLY** to serious matters

Ten words you are unlikely to have met before

1. **BRACHYGRAPHER.** One who can take and read shorthand.
2. **SYLLEPSIS.** A grammatical term for the use of a word in the same grammatical relation to two adjacent words, in its literal sense with one and metaphorical sense with the other. For example 'The gun fired, the ship and our hopes sank.' 'She left in tears and a taxi.' You can have a great deal of fun making them up.
3. **MUCKNA.** A male elephant with no tusks or only very small ones.
4. **UNDECENNIAL.** Lasting or happening every eleven years.
5. **RHIPIDATE.** Fan-like or fan-shaped.
6. **METAYER.** A farm-worker working for a share of the yield.
7. **GRAPHOSPASM.** Writer's cramp.
8. **EPANORTHOSIS.** Emphatic repetition.
9. **AVIGATION.** Aerial navigation.
10. **DELTIOLOGIST.** One who collects postcards.

Five strange things from the sea

1. **ELECTRIC EEL.** This is not an eel but a type of fish. Its claim to fame is its astonishing ability to discharge 500 volts at one ampere, which could kill a healthy man.

2. **BISEXUAL FISH.** Some fish can change sex but some, like the topminnow, are simultaneously male and female.

3. **THE KILLER CLAM.** This large and dangerous bivalve shell fish has the reputation for killing people, because a careless swimmer, who puts his hand or foot into the open shell, will find the shell shuts tight making it impossible to escape. If the victim is not rescued before the tide comes in, he will drown.

4. **JELLYFISH.** The most venomous animal in the world is the Chironex fleckeri, which grows on itself huge quantities of stinging cells. The stings can be fatal after only ten minutes.

5. **COELACANTH.** Fossil remains show that this fish existed 350,000,000 years ago. Present day specimens walk slowly about on the bottom of the Indian Ocean on four limb-fins and may well be the ancestors of four-limbed land creatures. The females produce the young already hatched.

Words often confused

1. **LIGHTENING** Making lighter. Making brighter.
   LIGHTNING A discharge of electricity in the atmosphere from cloud to cloud or cloud to earth and back.
2. **DELEGATION** A number of people sent to act as representatives.
   DELIGATION Bandaging, or a bandage.
3. **FLUOROID** A solid bounded by 24 triangular planes.
   FLUORIDE A binary compound of fluorine with another element.
4. **PRINCIPLE** As a noun means a law, a truth, a doctrine, a rule etc.
   PRINCIPAL One who is in charge. A head of a school. The leading actor in a play. Also a sum of money as distinct from the interest it acquires.
5. **URBAN** Relating to town or city.
   URBANE Well-bred. Elegant. Suave. (Yet from the same Latin root as 5A.)
6. **AFFECT** A verb meaning to influence.
   EFFECT A verb meaning to produce, accomplish, cause, complete, etc., and as a noun it means a result, or outcome.
7. **ALBUMEN** Egg white.
   ALBUMIN A class of *albuminoids* comprising those soluble in water, in dilute acids and alkalis.
8. **DEVISER** One who invents or devises something.
   DEVISOR One who disposes of property by means of a will.
   DIVISOR The number by which another number is divided.
9. **DOMINOS** Masks, especially thin black eye masks worn at fancy dress parties.
   DOMINOES Tiles with spots of a contrasting colour for playing games.
10. **UNORGANIZED** Not organized.
    DISORGANIZED Thrown into confusion.
11. **ANALYST** One who examines and lists the contents of a compound or mixture. One who can examine an argument, a statement etc.
    ANNALIST A chronicler, historian or recorder.
12. **BIANNUAL** Semi-annual, every six months.
    BIENNIAL Every other year. Once every two years.

Phrase origins

1. **'TO PETER OUT'** is a reference to Peter's behaviour after Jesus was taken from the Garden of Gethsemane, when Peter denied knowledge of him three times.
2. **'STARK NAKED'.** The word 'stark' is from the Anglo-Saxon word *steort* meaning rump or backside. So to be stark naked literally means 'with a bare bottom'.
3. **'TO PULL STRINGS'** is a reference to working a string puppet show. In other words, the doll on the stage is not in control.
4. **'TO PAY ON THE NAIL'** is to pay at once. In Mediaeval times a 'nail' was a shallow dish mounted on a stand. Seen from the distance it resembled a nail. As soon as a deal was settled, payment was made 'on the nail'. 'Nail' columns can still be seen outside the Corn Exchange in Bristol.
5. **'TO READ THE RIOT ACT.'** The Riot Act was introduced in 1761 and signed by George I. It was to stop riotous assembly, which was legally defined as a group of 12 or more people. Life imprisonment was one of the punishments given to anyone who broke this law.
6. **'FLAMING YOUTH'** is from William Shakespeare (Hamlet). 'To flaming youth let virtue be as wax, And melt in her own fire.'
7. **'STRAIGHT FROM THE HORSE'S MOUTH.'** This means that such information must be true. It is NOT a reference to horse racing as many think, but it refers to the only way to tell the age of a horse, which is by looking in its mouth at the teeth.
8. **'FIT TO A "T".'** This is from the T-square used by draughtsmen.
9. **'TO BE ON THE LEVEL.'** This means to be *straight* and *square*. This, and number '8', are supposedly terms from free-masonry.
10. **'HE IS POSH'.** Some books say this is from the expensive, shade-side cabins on the boats to India, when the rich would book Port Out Starboard Home. The clerk taking the booking would write P.O.S.H. against the traveller's name.

A list of crazed phrase

1. Money roots out all evil.
2. Never let a gift horse in the house.
3. None but the brave desert the fair.
4. People who live in glass houses shouldn't get stoned.
5. When it comes to giving, some stop at nothing.
6. A wolf in cheap clothing.
7. Be sincere, even when you don't mean it.
8. Mother's no's best.
9. The books arrived by partial post.
10. You can observe a lot by watching.

Reasons to stop smoking

Patti White, Information Officer to **ASH** (Action on Smoking and Health), sent me these two lists (see also page 66).

1. 90% of lung cancer deaths are attributable to smoking.
2. 90% of chronic bronchitis deaths are attributable to smoking.
3. 25% of coronary heart disease deaths are attributable to smoking.

4. Smokers have an increased risk of having cancer of the urinary tract, especially the bladder.
5. Smokers have an increased risk of having cancer of the mouth, throat and oesophagus.
6. 95% of patients with arterial disease of the legs, which may lead to gangrene of the leg — and subsequent amputation, are smokers.
7. Children whose parents smoke have more chest illnesses than those whose parents are non-smokers.
8. Still-births and deaths in the first week of life are nearly a third higher in babies whose mothers smoke.
9. Twice as many smokers as non-smokers produce babies weighing less than 2,500 grams.
10. Being with people who smoke is very uncomfortable for non-smokers, and recent evidence shows that it might be dangerous to them too.

11. The clothes and breath of smokers smell horrible. Heavy smokers have stained fingers. If you smoke, add up the daily cost, multiply it by 365 and there you have the amount of money you could spend on more interesting activities in one year.

Ways to stop smoking

Patti White gives this advice to those who are hooked and would like to stop.

1. **STOP** by yourself. There is no substitute for will power.
2. **STOP** with the help of leaflets and books.
3. **STOP** by using commercial preparations, such as mouth-wash, filters, etc.
4. **STOP** by joining a smoking withdrawal group.
5. **STOP** by using nicotine chewing gum.
6. **STOP** by using hypnosis.
7. **STOP** by taking a course of acupuncture.
8. **STOP** by cutting down.

Male and female differences

1. A woman's reflexes work ten times faster than those of a man: according to computers anyway.

2. Although there are more women in this world than men, all together they weigh fifteen percent less than all the men.
3. Cock parrots talk more than hen parrots.
4. Women can talk longer with less effort than men. Their vocal cords are shorter and need less breath to make the sound carry.
5. Women get drunk faster than men. Their bodies are about 58 per cent water, while men's bodies are about 70 per cent water which dilutes the alcohol more.
6. Man sings in the bath more than woman. The bathroom resonates better for him.
7. Women have better memories than men.
8. Knitting was a man's practice both as a hobby and for gain in the time of Henry VIII. After that much married king died, women started to knit.
9. Men change their minds more often than women.
10. More butchers in Finland are women than men.
11. Women can stand the rarified atmosphere of mountaineering better than men.
12. If a woman murders one of her family, it is more likely to happen in the kitchen, whereas if a man murders one of his family, it will probably be in the bedroom.
13. The female mosquito is the one to bite, not the male, and the same goes for the female horsefly.
14. In conversation out of doors, the man will not look at the woman, but the woman will frequently glance at the man.
15. The female kangaroo stops growing when she is adult. The male kangaroo continues to grow all his life.
16. Men have five times less warts than women.
17. Hospitals say that men fall out of bed twice as often as women.
18. Men are more 'red-blooded' than women. A count quickly shows that, with a man and woman of equal size, the man's red corpuscles outnumber the woman's.
19. When a woman buys flowers, she will buy any colour that takes her fancy at the moment, but the man will usually go for red: according to florists.
20. More men work for 'job satisfaction' than money. With the exception of nurses and girls with a 'calling', most women work only for the money.
21. More women get cross at being told they snore than do men accused of the same habit.

Notable dates in space exploration

Where space research remotely duplicates previous research, it has been left out for the sake of brevity. The following is mainly concerned with 'firsts'.

1. **1936** A USSR rocket rises to a height of 4.8 km (3 miles).
2. **1944** The German V-2, 15 metres (47 feet) long, 13.5 tons in weight (including the warhead of a ton) has a range of 320 km (200 miles).
3. **1946** A US launched V-2 rises from the White Sands Proving Ground in Mexico to a height of 183 km (114 miles).
4. **1957** On October 4, USSR launches Sputnik 1.
5. **1957** Sputnik II takes the first mammal, a dog called Laika, into space on November 3.
6. **1961** On April 12, Yury (sometimes *Yuri*) Gagarin makes a one orbit journey in the Russian craft Vostok I.
7. **1962** John Glenn, on 20 February, makes three orbits in Friendship 7 and in so doing becomes the first American in orbit.
8. **1965** A Russian space-walks for 10 minutes on March 18. An American makes a space walk on June 3.
9. **1966** A Russian unmanned craft makes a landing on the Moon and sends back information on January 31. The Russian Venera 3, which had been launched on November 11 the previous year, crashes on to Venus on March 1. On March 16, Gemini 8 with Americans Neil Armstrong and Dave Scott docks with unmanned Agena.
10. **1968** Three Americans in Apollo 8 make the first manned Moon flight and go round it 10 times.
11. **1969** Neil Armstrong becomes the first man on the Moon, followed by 'Buzz' Aldrin.
12. **1970** Russians land the first wheeled vehicle on the Moon on November 17. In the same year their Venera 7 arrives to soft land on Venus on December 15.
13. **1972** On March 3 the Americans launch the unmanned Pioneer 10 towards Jupiter some 1,000,000,000 km (620,000,000 miles) away.
14. **1973** On April 6, the US sends up Pioneer II to pass closer to Jupiter. The American Skylab I is launched.
15. **1974** Mariner 10 leaves us on a journey to take it *towards* the Sun.

16. **1975** On July 17, the Russian Soyuz 19 docks about 225 km (140 miles) above the Earth with the American Apollo 18. The crews of each ship exchange experiments.
17. **1976** Helios B, an American unmanned spacecraft, approaches within about 43,000,000 km (27,000,000 miles) of the Sun.
18. **1978** The unmanned Soviet Cosmos 954 breaks up in the atmosphere to spread itself over Canadian land. No one is hurt.
19. **1979** Two Russians spend a record 175 days in space. The unmanned US Skylab 1 breaks up in the atmosphere and spreads itself over Western Australia. No one is hurt.
20. **1980** Voyager 1 examines Saturn's rings from a distance of 126,000 km (78,000 miles) from the surface of the planet. Most of Venus is mapped by the Americans, who discover that the highest peak is 10,600 metres (34,000 feet).
21. **1981** The American shuttle, Columbia, proves itself by orbiting the Earth for 55 hours before gliding back to land on a desert strip.
22. **1984** Space Shuttle Challenger is launched February 3, 1984. The first unattached space walk is made by McCandless on Tuesday February 7, 1984. Space Shuttle Challenger lands safely on February 11.

Birthstones and flowers

BIRTHDAY IN	STONE	FLOWER
JANUARY	Garnet	Snowdrop
FEBRUARY	Amethyst	Primrose
MARCH	Aquamarine	Jonquil
APRIL	Diamond	Daisy
MAY	Emerald	Hawthorn
JUNE	Pearl	Rose
JULY	Ruby	Larkspur
AUGUST	Sardonyx	Poppy
SEPTEMBER	Sapphire	Aster
OCTOBER	Opal	Marigold
NOVEMBER	Topaz	Chrysanthemum
DECEMBER	Turquoise	Holly

Some of the morals of Aesop's fables

About 145 fables are credited to Aesop; here are some of the better known morals which he draws.

TITLE	MORAL
FOX AND THE CROW	Flatterers are not to be trusted.
GARDENER AND HIS DOG	Don't bite the hand that feeds you.
MILKMAID AND HER PAIL	Don't count your chickens before they hatch.
MICE IN COUNCIL (Bell the Cat)	It's one thing to propose, another to execute.
FOX AND GRAPES	Any fool can despise what he cannot get.
GOOSE WITH THE GOLDEN EGGS	The greedy, who want more, lose all.
HARE AND THE TORTOISE	Slow and steady wins the race.
ASS EATING THISTLES	One man's meat may be another man's poison.
JUPITER, NEPTUNE, MINERVA, AND MOMUS	It's time to criticize the works of others when you've done some good thing yourself.
BUNDLE OF STICKS	In union there is strength.
WOLF AND THE LAMB	Any excuse will serve a tyrant.
SHEPHERD BOY AND THE WOLF	Liars are not believed even when they tell the truth.

Reasons for sleeplessness

We asked 100 people what kept them awake and this is how they answered.

KEEPS ME AWAKE	%	KEEPS ME AWAKE	%
Worry	22	Snoring	18
Street noise (cars, etc.)	17	Coffee or tea	14
Rain/gales	8	Dogs barking	7
Baby	5	Neighbours' TV/Radio	4
Cats fighting	3	Nothing	2

Ten ways to save petrol

1. Keep your tyres at the correct pressure. This is also a safety measure. Check them once a week.
2. Tune or have your engine tuned frequently.
3. If you are not using a roof rack, take it off.
4. Remove all unnecessary items from the boot of the car.

5. Unless you live in a rural area with few petrol pumps, there is no need to fill your tank to the top each time. Petrol is heavy. 2 or 3 gallons are very light compared with 15 or 18 gallons.
6. Starting from cold, drive off as gently as possible and push the choke back in quickly.
7. Avoid driving fast up to a slow stream of traffic or a red light, because you will be wasting petrol when you have to brake hard. Touch your accelerator gently at all times.
8. Use the grade of petrol recommended for your car.
9. If the motorway limit is 70 mph, it does not follow that you must drive at that speed. Your car's cruising speed (see the handbook or telephone the maker) may be around 50 mph. If it is, stick to it as long as it is safe.
10. This is not by any means always possible, but avoid driving in heavy traffic. If you have to do it, turn the engine off, when you are at a standstill.

The cost of a railway ticket

T. J. Edgington, Information Officer of the National Railway Museum in York, sent this list of prices of the cost of a 3rd class (now 2nd Class) railway ticket from London to Birmingham. His letter says 'I am not sure we are doing a good P.R. job for them (British Rail) in view of the huge increases between 1970 and now.'

1890	9s 5d	47.5p (since 1846)
1900	9s 5d	47.5p
1910	9s 5d	47.5p
1920	16s 6d	82.5p
1930	14s 2d	71.0p
1940	15s 5d	77.0p
1950	£1-3s-0d	£1.15
1960	£1-3s-6d	£1.17½
1970	£1-14s-0d	£1.70
1980	£8.75p	
1983	£12.00	
1984	£12.70	

The seven sages

These Greeks all lived between 620 and 550 BC. Some were law givers and some just tyrants, however, they had two things in common, the ability to think, and towering personalities that were so impressive that their words have come down the centuries. Each one has left us with one wise saying.

SAGE	SAYING
1. CLEOBULUS OF RHODES.	Moderation is the chief good.
2. PERIANDER OF CORINTH.	Forethought in all things.
3. PITTACUS OF MITYLENE.	Know thine opportunity.
4. BIAS OF PRIENE.	Too many workers spoil the work.
5. THALES OF MILETUS.	Suretyship brings ruin.
6. CHILON OF SPARTA.	Know thyself.
7. SOLON OF ATHENS.	Nothing to excess.

Patron saints

SAINT	ASSOCIATED WITH FOOD AND DRINK
AUGUSTINE OF HIPPO	Brewers
LAWRENCE	Cooks
MARTHA	Dieticians
MICHAEL	Grocers
ARMAND	Inn keepers and wine merchants
VINCENT	Vineyard owners
NICHOLAS	Bakers

	ASSOCIATED WITH ENTERTAINMENT
GENESIUS	Actors
VITUS	Comedians
GREGORY	Musicians
CLARE	Television
GABRIEL	Radio

	ASSOCIATED WITH WRITING
BERNADINE OF SIENA	Advertising
FRANCIS DE SALES	Authors, journalists
JOHN BOSCO	Editors
JOHN OF GOD	Booksellers
DAVID	Poets
AUGUSTINE OF HIPPO	Printers (see also Brewers)
JEROME	Librarians

	ASSOCIATED WITH MEDICINE
APPOLLONIA	Dentists
CAMILLUS OF LELLIS	Nurses
PANTALEON	Physicians
COSMAS	Surgeons

And for good measure, while it is impossible to name all the saints, or, for that matter all the trades and professions, housewives may turn to ST ANNE, taxidrivers to ST FIACRE, carpenters to ST JOSEPH, students to ST THOMAS AQUINAS, bricklayers to ST STEPHEN and pawnbrokers to SANTA CLAUS, which is a corruption of the name ST NICHOLAS.

Hippo facts

1. A pregnant hippo gives birth under water.
2. The hippo is second only to the elephant in land mammal weight.
3. Hippos' stomachs can hold 8 bushels of grass.
4. Hippos' stomachs are 3.45 m (10 feet) long.
5. An angry hippo appears to sweat blood, because it sweats a red mucus through its skin. The same happens if it stays out of water too long.
6. A hippo can open its mouth 1.35 m (4 feet) wide.
7. Hippopotamus means 'river horse' but it is a close relative of the pig.
8. Using a normal rifle bullet it is not possible to shoot a hippo through its skin because it is so thick.
9. A man cannot run as fast as a hippo.

10. A hippo is a vegetarian but if a man makes him angry and the hippo catches him, the hippo can bite him in half.
11. Totally submerged hippos often walk about on the bottom of the river or pool they live in.
12. André Simon, possibly the world's greatest literary chef wrote that '(the hippo) has been eaten and declared fairly good eating by Puleston and other travellers.

Interesting happenings in 1884

As this book is published in 1984, this list goes back exactly 100 years to find out what people were talking about in 1884.

1. The pop song of the day is **'There's a Tavern in the Town'** published the previous year (USA), but with no radio, etc., songs take time to grow on people.
2. The first performance of **Ibsen's** (Norwegian) **'Wild Duck'** is seen.
3. **Gordon** (UK) reaches Khartoum.
4. **Edgar Dégas** (French), one of the greatest draftsmen in the history of western art, exhibits his two pastels 'The Ironers' and 'Café Singers'.
5. **The Berlin conference** of 14 nations on African affairs institutes free trade on the Congo (Zaire) River and the abolition of the Slave Trade.
6. The Paris newspaper **'Le Matin'** is launched.
7. **Sean O'Casey** (Irish) is born. (d.1964).
8. The first practical **steam turbine** is constructed by **Sir Charles Parsons** (UK) and used for generating electricity.
9. **Divorce**, which had been abolished in France in 1816, is re-established.
10. **Rodin** (French) sculpts the **'Burghers of Calais'**.
11. The **Fabian Society** is founded.
12. **Goldsmith Fabergé** (French) makes the first jewelled egg for the Tzar of Russia.
13. The first deep **underground railway** is constructed under London.
14. USA establishes **Pearl Harbor** as a naval base.
15. **Bangor** (N.Wales) **University College** is founded.
16. **Gold** is discovered in the Transvaal in South Africa and gives birth to the town of **Johannesburg.**
17. **Peter Tchaikovsky** (Russian) writes **'Mazeppa'**, the opera.
18. The **Revised Version of the Old Testament** is published.
19. **Georges Seurat**, (French) noted for painting with small dots of pure colour which from a distance appear to blend, paints **'Une Baignade, Asnières'**.
20. **Martial Law** is declared in **Austria** to check anarchists.
21. **The 3rd English Reform Act** extends the franchise to farm workers.
22. Russians seize **Merv** in Turkestan.

Left overs

1. Painter Vincent van Gogh cut off part of his LEFT ear.
2. At the end of the LEFT arm of the Captain Hook in Peter Pan was his dreaded hook.
3. Sammy Davis Jr's LEFT eye is glass.
4. Most women wear their wedding rings on their LEFT hand.
5. Captain Ahab's LEFT leg was bitten off by Moby Dick and replaced with an ivory one.
6. The cane carried by Charlie Chaplin was in his LEFT hand.
7. Long John Silver lost his LEFT leg.
8. A horse is usually mounted on the LEFT side.
9. Ladies who wear skirts that have zippers will tell you that the zipper is usually on the LEFT side.
10. The first foot that stood on the moon was Armstrong's LEFT foot.

Words etcetera

1. In most (but not all) languages, the word for Mother starts with an 'M' sound.
2. A letter check of this book with a computer shows that the letter E has been used most and the letter Q has been used least.
3. Only one word sounds the same before and after the last four letters have been chopped off – QUEUE.
4. Because of an ancient Japanese custom of never referring to great men directly, the word MIKADO meant a door. Not any door – only the door to the M. . . .'s royal residence.
5. A GOOGOL is this number:
   10,000,000,000,000,000,000,000,000,000,000,000,000,000,000,000,000,000,000,000,000,000,000,000,000,000,000,000,000,000,000,000,000,000,000,000. (And if you don't want to count the 0s there are 100 of them.)
6. Write the words CHOICE COD in capital letters and hold it upside-down to read it in the mirror. You may be surprised.
7. If you ask an Eskimo the word for SNOW, he can give you any one of 20 words, all meaning SNOW.
8. This is an ampersand – &. It was at one time a letter of the alphabet.

9. Fairground sellers of dubious medicines which cured everything, once used assistants who would eat toads alive to draw the crowds. Toads were also considered deadly poisonous. The assistant would fake his own death and the 'professor' would use his wonder-cure to revive him from death itself. Sales were therefore assured. This has given our language the word TOADY.

10. A ball of wool was once known as a 'CLUE'. That is why clues have to be unravelled, not solved.

Words with their origins in names

1. **AARON'S ROD.** A plant, a type of *solidago* commonly called Golden Rod.

2. **ABIGAIL.** A maidservant. From Nabal's wife in the Old Testament who appeased David and his following (after they had been slighted by her husband) by supplying them with provisions.

3. **ALBERT.** A watch-chain. After Prince Albert.

4. **DENIM.** Short for 'serge de Nimes'. Cloth from Nimes, a place in the south of France.

5. **DANDY.** From Dandy, a nickname meaning Andrew.

6. **CHESTERFIELD.** A large well-stuffed sofa. Named after the Earl of Chester.

7. **CHAUVINIST.** An excessive patriot. From Nicholas Chauvin of Rochefort, France, a veteran of the 1st Republic, whose exaggerated patriotism was ultimately ridiculed by his colleagues.

8. **BOBBY.** A policeman. Nickname from Sir Robert Peel, Home Secretary 1828.

9. **JOCKEY.** One who rides in horse races. From the Scottish Jock, or Jack.

10. **TEDDY-BEAR.** From Theodore (Teddy) Roosevelt who, when president of the USA, refused to shoot a bear because he preferred to spare its life.

11. **CRISS-CROSS.** From Christ's Cross.

12. **PASTEURIZE.** From Louis Pasteur the French scientist.

13. **HESSIAN.** Coarse cloth originally made in Hesse, Germany.

14. **GAMP.** An umbrella, from Sarah Gamp, a disreputable nurse in Dicken's *Martin Chuzzlewit*, who always carried one.

Facts about your skin

1. Your skin kills germs at faster than 1,500 a second.
2. You pick up germs at about one and a quarter million an hour.
3. If you are fit, you control your body temperature so efficiently that it will not change by so much as a degree whether you are on the Equator or at the North Pole.
4. When you are hot on the outside, each of your pores releases perspiration to cool you in much the same way a steam engine will release its safety valve to prevent over heating.
5. When you are cold on the outside your skin insulates you by using oil glands to make you waterproof.
6. The skin on the bottom of your feet is about ½ cm (¼ inch) thick.
7. The skin on your eyelid is the thinnest surface skin you have and is about 1 mm (¹⁄₂₄ inch) thick.
8. Your skin pigment protects you from the rays of the sun and when exposed to strong rays will discolour. That is what suntan is.
9. Every time you wash you take off one layer of skin. But you keep replacing it from below, so you can never wash yourself away.
10. Washing is good for you. It keeps the skin clean, so that the acids in the skin glands can rise to the surface and kill germs.

Words most used in conversation

This word count was taken from a recording of a sixty minute BBC discussion programme. This in descending order is the frequency with which each word was used.

1.	I	2.	AND
3.	ME	4.	YOU
5.	YES	6.	THE
7.	A	8.	BUT
9.	WHAT	10.	LIKE
11.	WELL	12.	THAT
13.	NO	14.	DO

Ten printed items that made me laugh

1. A hotel in Spain displayed this message in all bedrooms 'CLOTHES MUST NOT BE WASHED IN THE HAND BASIN AND WHEN THEY ARE THEY MUST NOT BE HUNG OUT TO DRY ON THE BALCONY.'
2. A chemist in Birmingham 'WE DISPENSE WITH ACCURACY.'
3. Nottingham barbershop 'HAIR CUT WHILE YOU WAIT.'

4. On the label of a bottle of shampoo '. . . pour a little into the palm of each hand.'
5. A New York paper '. . . so the President was surrounded by the tightest possible security officers. . .'
6. Advertisement in East Kent Mercury 'ONCE YOU HAVE DEALT WITH US YOU WILL RECOMMEND OTHERS.'
7. Newfoundland paper '. . . what first attracted him to her was the way she flashed her sensationally deep blue ewes. . .'
8. A Do-It-Yourself magazine '. . . as soon as you have cut the 3 inch diameter holes in the cabinet door, be sure to sand and varnish them before attaching the hinges.'
9. Astrological magazine '. . . take good care to avoid unforeseen troubles. . .'
10. A romance magazine '. . . she worried about the way he felt about her. . .'

Real but sometimes unfortunate names of people

1. In Bridgnorth (Salop) there is a firm of solicitors by the name of **DOOLITTLE AND DALLY**.
2. There is a firm of Birmingham undertakers called **de'ATH**.
3. 'General' Tom Thumb, the 100 cm (40 inch) tall midget who was given the title 'General' by Queen Victoria, married another midget called **MERCY BUMPUS**.
4. In Westminster Abbey is the grave of, and extravagant memorial to, an admiral of the Royal Navy who ran his fleet aground on some rocks near the Scilly Isles in 1707. Over 2,000 of his own men were drowned. His name was Sir **CLOUDSLEY SHOVEL**.
5. According to Chamber's Biographical Dictionary, there was a theological writer born at Seville of an Irish Catholic family in 1775 and died in 1841 whose name was **BLANCO WHITE**.
6. In 'A History of Piracy' you will find a pirate born in Falmouth with the name of **ARISTOTLE TOTTLE**.
7. In Johannesburg lives a man by the name of **ICECREAM SUNDAY**.
8. There is a NASA computer programmer by the name of **I. BANG**.
9. Having read this in three different accounts I am inclined to believe it, but it is unsubstantiated. In Victoria, British Columbia there is a singing teacher by the name of **MRS. SCREECH**.
10. There are TWO ladies in London named **PRIMROSE HILL**.

Biblical forties

1. It rained for 40 days and nights.
2. Moses spent 40 days and nights on the mountain.
3. Israel was in the wilderness for 40 years.
4. Elijah was in the wilderness for 40 days and nights.
5. Nineveh was given 40 days to repent.
6. Christ was in the wilderness for 40 days and nights.
7. Lent lasts for 40 days and nights.
8. 'Five times I received 40 stripes save one.'
   (II Corinthians.)

Words often used incorrectly

The incorrect word or phrase will be in capitals. If you are not sure why they are wrong, look for them in your dictionary.

1. Drunken drivers should be treated with extra **VIGOUR**.
   For **VIGOUR** read **RIGOUR**.
2. The school girls' gymnastic display showed how **VIRILE** they were. For **VIRILE** read **ENERGETIC**.
3. The music **INSTILLED** the audience with national pride.
   For **INSTILLED** read **IMBUED**.
4. Do you really **EVER HOPE** to succeed?
   For **EVER HOPE** read **HOPE EVER**.
5. Women **SUPERSEDE** men in driving skills.
   For **SUPERSEDE** read **SURPASS**.
6. Next time you will try **AND** do it better.
   For **AND** read **TO**.
7. The water took up a larger **PERCENTAGE** of the space in the bowl than the stones and fish.
   For **PERCENTAGE** read **PROPORTION**.
8. They could not find him, but knew he must be some **PLACE**.
   For some **PLACE** read some**WHERE**. ˙
9. **THEY EACH** did something towards the barbecue.
   For **THEY EACH** read **EACH OF THEM**.
10. The doctor mixed his special **PANACEA** for colds.
    For **PANACEA** use **MEDICINE** or **REMEDY**.
11. The men were engaged in **CALLISTHENICS**.
    For **CALLISTHENICS** use **GYMNASTICS** or possibly **AEROBICS** (through common usage, although no such word as AEROBIC exists in the Oxford English Dictionary. It is in Webster's meaning 1. Taking place in the presence of oxygen. 2. Living or active only in the presence of oxygen).

Odd mammal facts

1. A camel can go thirsty for a week and do without food for a fortnight.
2. You can distinguish between about 200 colours.
3. A bloodhound can detect some scents up to nine days old.
4. Portuguese explorers of South America took convicts to send ashore ahead of them to check whether the local inhabitants were cannibals.
5. A whale can weigh over a hundred tons. A mouse can weigh a couple of ounces. In spite of this they both develop from eggs almost the same size.
6. The Carthaginians named a rabbit-infested land, Spania, meaning 'land of rabbits'. This land is now known as Spain.
7. If you have two cups of tea when you wake up, two more with your breakfast, and two more during the afternoon or evening, you will drink 2,190 cups of tea a year.
8. The gestation period of an elephant is 21 months.
9. The dingo dog of Australia can play possum better than the possum. It will pretend to be dead even allowing itself to be beaten unmercifully. Then, when the chance comes, it will jump up and escape.
10. Of the 38 best known breeds of horse, 16 started in these islands.

Eleven cities furthest by air from the UK

To the nearest 100 miles and 50 km.

1.	**AUCKLAND**	18,350 km	11,400 miles
2.	**SYDNEY**	17,050 km	10,600 miles
3.	**BRISBANE**	16,550 km	10,300 miles
4.	**PERTH**	14,450 km	9,000 miles
5.	**DARWIN**	13,850 km	8,600 miles
6.	**HONOLULU**	11,600 km	7,200 miles
7.	**SINGAPORE**	10,950 km	6,800 miles
8.	**KUALA LUMPUR**	10,600 km	6,600 miles
9.	**MAURITIUS**	9,800 km	6,100 miles
10.	**HONG KONG**	9,650 km	6,000 miles
11.	**TOKYO**	9,650 km	6,000 miles

A list about the lie detector
And why its results are doubtful.

1. It cannot distinguish between fact and fiction.
2. Instead, it draws a wavy line which has to be translated.
3. This leaves its 'results' in the hands of the one who prepared the questions. A lot has to be known about the speaker before the analyser can make a pronouncement.
4. The test must not last more than about three minutes.
5. The questions must be put in such a way that they can be answered 'yes' or 'no'.
6. The resulting movements of the stylus drawing the graph depend on the subject's blood pressure, breathing, pulse and skin moisture. Thus the machine must be suspect, because many of us blush when accused of something disgraceful even when innocent.
7. Many criminals are from a background which does not allow them to take advantage of all the subtleties of our language. If they fail to comprehend the questions they will not react normally.
8. As the circumstances of using a lie detector can force up blood pressure, etc., this in itself should put it out of court.

Coal prices

This list of dates and coal prices has been kindly researched for us by Charringtons Solid Fuel (Charringtons Fuels Ltd) with J. A. Spiegel, Managing Director. He points out that the curious rise in 1920 and subsequent fall was due to the shortage of manpower after the First World War. In his letter he adds that the prices 'took some finding'. And if you have ever had to research archives you will know what he means. The prices varied over the UK, so this list relates only to:

PRICE PER TONNE OF HOUSE COAL DELIVERED IN THE LONDON AREA

1890	£1.00
1900	£1.30
1910	£1.30
1920	£3.00
1930	£2.50
1940	£2.60
1950	£5.50
1960	£10.00
1970	£19.00
1980	£80.00
1984	£102.00

The ten most popular package deal continental holiday resorts

1. BENIDORM (Spain)
2. CORFU (Greece)
3. LLORET DE MAR (Spain)
4. MAGALLUF (Majorca)
5. SAN ANTONIO (Ibiza)
6. SALOU (Spain)
7. TORREMOLINOS (Spain)
8. PARIS (France)
9. PALMA NOVA (Majorca)
10. CALELLA (Spain)

Our solar system planets

These are the known planets in order from the Sun outwards. There may also be a minor planet inside the orbit of Mercury, which until now has always been assumed to be the one closest to the Sun. As no planet describes an absolute circle round the Sun, the mean distance is given. By the time you read this the number of moons for a given planet may, because of space exploration, have increased.

MERCURY
Mean distance from Sun: 58,000,000 km or 36,250,000 miles.
One Mercurian year is equal to 89 Earth days.
One day is equal to about 60 Earth days (variable).
Speed of travel round Sun: 2,880 km or 1,800 miles a minute.
Maximum diameter: 4,868 km or 3,050 miles.
No moons.
Not on view except in the early morning or late evening.
Life, certainly as we know it, is out of the question.

VENUS
Mean distance from Sun: 107,500,000 km or 67,200,000 miles.
One Venusian year is equal to 225 Earth days.
One day, during which it rotates in the opposite direction to the other planets, is equal to about 245 Earth days (variable), so a day there is longer than its year.
Speed of travel round the Sun: about 2,100 km (1,740 miles) a minute.
Maximum diameter of the solid (excluding clouds and gases): about 12,300 km or 7,663 miles.
No moons.
Life as we know it is not possible.

EARTH
Mean distance from Sun: 150,000,000 km (93,000,000 miles).
One year is roughly 365¼ days and adjustments have to be made in the calendar to allow for the variations.
One day is about 23 hours, 56 minutes, 4.09 secs.
Speed of travel round the Sun: about 1,800 km (1,100 miles) a minute.
Maximum (equatorial) diameter: 12,756.4 km (7,925.4 miles).
One moon.

MARS
Mean distance from Sun: 227,800,000 km (142,000,000 miles).
One Martian year is equal to 1.88 Earth years.
One day on Mars lasts 24 hours and 39 minutes.
Maximum diameter: 6,890 km (4,219 miles).
Two moons: Phobos (fear) and Deimos (panic).
Life has not yet been discovered on the surface.

JUPITER
Mean distance from Sun: 778,000,000 km (484,000,000 miles).
One Jupiter year is equal to 11.86 Earth years.
A day on Jupiter at the equator is only 9 hours and 50 minutes.
Diameter at the Equator: 143,200 km (88,930 miles).
Thirteen moons: Amalthea, Io, Europa, Ganymede, Callistro, Leda, Himalia, Lysithea, Elara, Ananke, Carme, Pasiphae and Sinope.

SATURN
Mean distance from Sun: 1,427,000,000 km (887,000,000 miles).
One year on Saturn is equivalent to 29.46 years on Earth.
One day on Saturn is equivalent to 10 hours and 14 minutes at the Equator.
Nine moons: Mimas, Enceladus, Tethys, Dione, Rhea, Titan, Hyperion, Iapetus and Phoebe.
The rings have been studied since the days of Galileo.
(See also page 49).

URANUS
Mean distance from Sun: 2,870,000,000 km (1,783,000,000 miles).
One year lasts 84 of our years.
A day there lasts 10 hours and 49 minutes.
Five moons: Miranda, Ariel, Umbriel, Titania and Oberon.
Equatorial diameter: 47,100 km (29,300 miles).
This planet also has rings round it: about 8, possibly more.

NEPTUNE
Mean distance from Sun: 4,497,000,000 km (2,794,000,000 miles).
It takes 164.97 years to go round the Sun.
One day on Neptune lasts 15 hours and 8 minutes.

Maximum diameter: 50,950 km (31,700 miles) including the atmosphere.
Two moons: Triton and Nereid.

PLUTO
Mean distance from Sun: 5,590,000,000 km (3,697,000,000 miles).
One year on Pluto lasts the equivalent of 248.5 of our years.
It takes 6.39 days to turn on its axis.
Diameter: roughly 5,000 km (3,750 miles).
One moon: Charon.

PLANET X
It is possible that beyond Pluto is another planet.
Little is known of it yet and for that reason it has been called X.

Place names that do not look as they sound

NAME	LOOKS LIKE	SHOULD BE PRONOUNCED
FOWEY	Phooey	Foy
MOUSEHOLE	Mouse hole	Mouzel
BELVOIR	Bell Voyeur	Beaver
LYMPNE	Limp knee	Limm
BALQUHIDDER	Bal-Q-Hidder	Balhwidder
LEOMINSTER	Leo Minster	Lemster
ZWILL	Szwill	Yool
ULGHAM	Ul-ger-ham	Uffam
KIRCUDBRIGHT	Kerr-Cud-Brite	Kerkoobri
BEAUCHAMP	Bow Champ	Beecham
ST. JOHN	Saint John	Sinjun
CONDUIT	Kon-du-it	Cundit
BICESTER	Bye Cester	Bister
CIRENCESTER	Siren Sester	Sissister (But this is dying out)
LEICESTER	Lie Sester	Lester
WYMONDHAM	Why-mond-ham	Windum
HUNSTANTON	Hun-stan-ton	Hunston

Weekday births according to old superstition

Monday's child is fair of face.
Tuesday's child is full of grace.
Wednesday's child is full of woe.
Thursday's child has far to go.
Friday's child is loving and giving.
Saturday's child works hard for a living.
But the child that is born on the **Sabbath** day
Is blithe and bonny, good and gay.

Seven deadly sins

These were grouped by St Gregory the Great in the 6th century AD. Of them, Thomas Aquinas said 'deadly because each gives rise to others. . .'

1. PRIDE.
2. COVETOUSNESS.
3. LUST.
4. ENVY.
5. GLUTTONY.
6. ANGER.
7. IDLENESS.

Ten old and still popular indoor games
(Excluding card games which are too varied and numerous.)

1. **CHESS:** Most likely origin — fifth century India.

2. **DRAUGHTS:** Developed from a version played in 1600 BC by the pharaohs.

3. **PACHISI:** National game of India — called 'ludo' in this country.

4. **DOMINOES:** Invented in the thirteenth century by the Chinese.

5. **BACKGAMMON:** Devised by an Indian, originally called 'tables', played by Nero.

6. **NINE MEN'S MORRIS:** Found inscribed on the roof of the temple of Kurma in Egypt, carved by builders in 1400 BC.

7. **FOX AND GEESE:** A forerunner of 'Solitaire', boards dating from the thirteenth century have been found in Russia, Sweden, Italy and Ireland.

8. **SOLITAIRE:** Developed from 'Fox and Geese' by a French nobleman in the 1790s, to while away his time in the Bastille.

9. **DICE:** Found in Egyptian tombs dating back to 2000 BC.

10. **ROULETTE:** First seen in France under the name of *Hoca* in about 1655.

UK caves worth visiting

There are more undiscovered caves in the UK than those we know about. If you are not an expert caver, or speleologist, it is unwise to go to a cave where you have to crawl or squeeze yourself through narrow openings. There are some 40 large *known* caves in these lands, of which about 30 are safe, artificially lit, and are shown by a helpful guide.

1. **CHEDDAR GORGE, SOMERSET.** Special attraction — Cox's Cave.

2. **WOOKEY HOLE CAVES, SOMERSET.** Special attraction — Goatsherd Chamber, Witch's Parlour, and Witch's Kitchen.

3. **WHITE SCAR CAVE, INGLETON, YORKSHIRE.** Special attraction — stalactites, underground river and waterfall.

4. **ST CLEMENT'S CAVES, HASTINGS, SUSSEX.** Special attraction — they were once a gamblers' haunt.

5. **WEST WYCOMBE CAVES, WEST WYCOMBE, BUCKINGHAMSHIRE.** Special attraction — waxwork effigies, taped commentary and the 'Inner Temple'.

6. **REDCLIFFE CAVES, BRISTOL.** Special attraction — maze of caves with extensive history.

7. **CATHEDRAL CAVE, PEN-Y-CAE, BRECONSHIRE.** Special attraction — brilliant illuminations.

8. **SPEEDWELL CAVERN, CASTLETON, DERBYSHIRE.** Special attraction — underground boat trip.

9. **BRUCE'S CAVE, KIRKPATRICK FLEMING, DUMFRIES AND GALLOWAY.** Special attraction — Robert Bruce was stuck here, watching the famous spider.

10. **ROYSTON CAVE, ROYSTON, HERTFORDSHIRE.** Special attraction — ancient wall sculptures.

A UK numerical place names list

1. **ONCE BREWED.** At Hadrian's Wall near Haltwhistle, 3 kilometres (2 miles) off the A 69.
2. **TWO BRIDGES.** Devon. At the junction of the B3212 and the B3357.
3. **THREE COCKS.** Powys. At the junction of the A438 and the A4079.
4. **FOUR ASHES.** About 3 kilometres (2 miles) north of Wolverhampton by Junction 12 of the M6, and not 3 kilometres (2 miles) to the north east is **FOUR CROSSES** on the north side of the A5.
5. **FIVE PENNY BORVE.** On the island of Lewis on the A857, and 13½ kilometres (8½ miles) away is **FIVE PENNY NESS.**
6. **SIXPENNY HANDLEY.** Dorset. On the B3081, about 19 kilometres (12 miles) west south west of Salisbury.
7. **SEVEN BRIDGES.** Wiltshire. On the A419 about 9½ kilometres (6 miles) north west of Swindon.
8. **EIGHT ASH GREEN.** Suffolk. Near the A12 about 5 kilometres (3 miles) due west of Colchester.
9. **NINE MILE BURN.** Lothian. On the A702 about 21 kilometres (13 miles) south south west of Edinburgh.
10. **TEN MILE BANK.** Cambridgeshire. Just off the A10 about 22½ kilometres (14 miles) south of King's Lynn.

Mazes and labyrinths

Mazes have come and gone from antiquity to the present day. Should you find yourself in a typical maze with no detached walls, it is easy to find the middle and the way out. Just extend one hand (say the left hand) and touch that wall. Keep touching that wall until you have found the middle — and you will find it. Use the same method to find your way out. This is not necessarily the shortest way but it is foolproof.

1. **The Clusium Labyrinth** — built to conceal the tomb of the King of Etruria, Lars Porsena.
2. **The Cretan Labyrinth** — built to house the dreadful Minotaur.
3. **The Egyptian Labyrinth** — probably a temple, at Crocodilopolis, east of Moeris.
4. **The Lemnian Labyrinth** — similar to the Egyptian labyrinth.
5. **Cathedral mazes** — The following French cathedrals have very fine mazes in the floors: Abbey of St Berlin at St. Omer, Sens Cathedral, Poitiers Cathedral, Bayeux Cathedral, Amiens Cathedral, Chartres Cathedral and Rheims Cathedral.
6. **Hampton Court Maze** — planted at the end of the 17th century.
7. **Somerlyton Hall**, Lowestoft — laid out in yew hedges by John Thomas in 1897.
8. **Theobald's Park Maze,** Cheshunt — existed at the time of James I.
9. **Wimbledon House Maze** — existed in 1750 at the seat of the Earl Spencer.
10. **Susa Tomb Mosaic** — in the form of an intricate maze, due south of Tunis.

Ten remarkable castles

BERKSHIRE

1. **Donnington Castle**, near Newbury — built by a knight of the Black Prince, Richard de Adderbury in about 1250.
2. **Windsor Castle** — the biggest castle in the British Isles. Built by William the Conquerer, much added to since, last addition the chapel built as a memorial to George VI.

CHESHIRE

3. **Chester Castle** – built by the sixth Earl of Chester on a 160 m (500 ft) rock of sandstone in about 1230.

CORNWALL

4. **St Michael's Mount** – looks very similar to Mont St. Michel in France and was linked spiritually with it in about 1000 AD, when it became a Benedictine monastery.

5. **Tintagel** – now no more than a broken down ruin, but once possibly housed the Court of King Arthur.

KENT

6. **Leeds** castle – built by the Saxons, is confusingly named because it is nowhere near Leeds. It stands in the middle of a lake on 3 islands connected by bridges. It has been a prison for several people including Richard II, Henry IV's wife, and his aunt, who was condemned to stay there all her life after she had been proved to be a witch.

7. **Hever Castle** near Edenbridge – built by Sir John de Cobham in 1384, preserved by the 1st Viscount Astor, who took it over in 1903 and being a most sociable man built a village for his guests in the grounds.

SHROPSHIRE

8. **Stokesay** – built by a rich wool merchant in about 1290. It passed down through the family peacefully and was sold twice, but Royalist Lord Craven, who bought it just before the Civil War was forced to surrender it.

SUSSEX

9. **Arundel Castle** – first occupied by the Duke of Norfolk in 1580, much restored, rebuilding completed in 1716 by the 15th Duke of Norfolk.

CAERNARVONSHIRE

10. **Caernarvon Castle** – building began in 1283, now associated with the investiture of the Prince of Wales.

The ten longest rivers in round figures

RIVER	LENGTH Kilometres (Miles)	FLOWS INTO
1. NILE	6,640 (4,150)	Mediterranean
2. AMAZON	6,240 (3,900)	Atlantic
3. MISSISSIPPI-MISSOURI-RED ROCK	6,080 (3,800)	Gulf of Mexico
4. YANGTZE	5,440 (3,400)	North Pacific
5. OB-IRTYSH	5,120 (3,200)	Arctic
6. HWANG-HO	4,640 (2,900)	North Pacific
7. CONGO	4,640 (2,900)	Atlantic
8. AMUR	4,480 (2,800)	North Pacific
9. LENA	4,480 (2,800)	Arctic
10. MEKONG	4,480 (2,800)	China Sea

Drivers' statements after an accident

These are genuine statements made in writing to an insurance company, collected by John Ackley. The forms state clearly that the drivers MUST summarize the details as briefly as possible.

1. Coming home I drove into the wrong house and collided with a tree I didn't have.
2. The other car collided with mine without giving warning of its intention.
3. I thought my window was down, but I found it was up when I put my head through it.
4. I collided with a stationary lorry coming the other way.
5. A van backed through the windscreen and into my wife's face.
6. A pedestrian hit me and went under my car.
7. The man was all over the road, I had to swerve a number of times before I hit him.
8. I looked at my mother-in-law, and headed over the embankment.
9. I had been driving for 40 years when I fell asleep and had an accident.

10. In my attempt to kill a fly, I drove into a telephone pole.
11. I was on my way to the doctor with rear end trouble when my universal joint gave way causing me to have an accident.
12. To avoid hitting the bumper of the car in front, I struck the pedestrian.
13. As I approached the intersection, a sign suddenly appeared in a place where no stop sign had ever appeared before. I was unable to stop in time to avoid the accident.
14. My car was legally parked as it backed into the other vehicle.
15. An invisible car came out of nowhere, struck my car and vanished.

16. I told the police that I was not injured, but on removing my hat, I found I had a fractured skull.
17. I was sure the old fellow would never make to the other side of the road when I struck him.
18. The pedestrian had no idea which direction to run, so I ran over him.
19. The telephone pole was approaching. I was attempting to swerve out of its way when it struck the front end.
20. I saw a slow moving, sad old gentleman as he bounced off the roof of my car.

A list of fatal accidents

This list, while not given in percentages, is of killer-dangers you can meet in your own home in descending order of frequency.

1. **FALLS** account for the greatest number of deaths especially for those over 65.
2. **FIRE.**
3. **ACCIDENTAL POISONING.**
4. **ELECTROCUTION.** (Damp hands, damp feet and press an improperly fitted electric switch.)
5. **CHOKING ON FOOD.**

Feminist proposals

Most thinking people believe in equal pay for men and women doing the same work, and that women should not be barred from a trade or profession because they are women. Many feel, however, that there are some who have taken feminism a stage too far. The following are all proposals that have been seriously put forward **on more than one occasion**.

1. The Lord's Prayer should not be so male oriented and should follow these lines: 'Our Person which art in Heaven etc.'
2. At the end of matins the vicar (or whatever the word would be for his female counterpart) should say 'Glory be to the Person, and to the Person's Child and the Holy Ghost...'
3. Consider starting the Creed with 'I believe in God, the Person Almighty, maker of Heaven and Earth....'
4. Person Christmas or at least as many Mother Christmases as Father Christmases.
5. Abolish man-eating tigers. They will all be person-eating tigers.
6. Serious thought has been given in at least one town to changing the name of those holes in the street from manholes to personholes.
7. The all-embracing term 'mankind' should be changed to 'personkind'.
8. The plant 'mandrake' takes its name from its appearance being similar to a human being, so it should be a 'persondrake'.

9. The word 'manhandle' should be changed to 'personhandle'.
10. 'Manslaughter' should become 'personslaughter'.

World times

Use this to find out the time in another country, so that you don't mistakenly phone your friends in Melbourne at 3 in the morning (their time). This is not totally straightforward, however, due to the variations between British Summer Time and Daylight Saving Schemes which some other countries also have. The guide is mostly accurate in winter. The time given will be based on GMT in each case.

12.00 GMT IN THE UK

ALGIERS **1.00** PM
ATHENS **2.00** PM
BEIRUT **2.00** PM
BERLIN **1.00** PM
BOMBAY **5.30** PM
BUCHAREST **2.00** PM
BUENOS AIRES **9.00** AM
CALCUTTA **5.30** PM
CHICAGO **6.00** AM
HELSINKI **2.00** PM
ISTANBUL **3.00** PM
KARACHI **5.00** PM
LIMA **7.00** PM
MADRAS **5.00** PM
MELBOURNE **2.00** AM
NEW YORK **7.00** AM
PARIS **1.00** PM
ROME **1.00** PM
SINGAPORE **8.00** PM
TOKYO **9.00** PM

AMSTERDAM **1.00** PM
AUCKLAND **12.00** midnight
BELGRADE **1.00** PM
BERNE **1.00** PM
BRUSSELS **1.00** PM
BUDAPEST **1.00** PM
CAIRO **2.00** PM
CAPE TOWN **2.00** PM
COPENHAGEN **1.00** PM
HONG KONG **8.00** PM
JERUSALEM **2.00** PM
LAGOS **1.00** PM
LISBON **12.00** midday
MADRID **1.00** PM
MOSCOW **3.00** PM
OSLO **1.00** PM
PEKING **8.00** PM
SAN FRANCISCO **4.00** AM
SYDNEY **10.00** PM
WARSAW **1.00** PM

Ornithological oddities

1. **PENGUINS.** Penguins stay with one partner all their adult lives. Parents so love their own offspring that they will starve to death rather than let the chicks starve.

2. **PENCULINE TITMOUSE.** The nests of this African bird are so strong that some people use them for carrier bags.
3. **HUMMING BIRDS.** Some humming birds beat their wings at 80 strokes to the second (which is why they hum), weigh about the same as a 20p piece, and can fly backwards.
4. **OSTRICHES.** One ostrich egg can be turned into 10 good-sized omelettes.
5. **PETRELS.** Do not corner a petrel (which lives in the Antarctic). It will be frightened and you will be subjected to a horrible experience. It will either throw up over you or it will squirt oil from its nostrils, so hard it can knock you over. Sometimes it will do both.
6. **HARPY EAGLES.** Monkeys are a favourite food of the South American harpy eagle.
7. **FLAMINGOES.** Flamingoes are naturally pink, but will lose their colour if deprived of a green algae which they eat without realizing it.

8. **DUCKS.** You will never see a duck lay an egg in the evening. No one knows why but they lay only in the morning.
9. **ALBATROSSES.** Sea water does not damage the albatross, which drinks nothing else, because its digestive tract takes out most of the salt.
10. **BIRD BATHS.** The water in a bird bath should be about 6 cm (2½ inches) deep: more will worry the birds, less makes it difficult for them.

Unusual UK place names

These places were found by Lyn and Kate Goldberg.

1. **UGLEY.** Suffolk. About 6 kilometres (4 miles) north of Bishop's Stortford just off the west side of the M11.
2. **GREAT SNORING.** Norfolk. About 5½ kilometres (3½ miles) north of Fakenham, and using that road to get there will take you close to **LITTLE SNORING**.
3. **YELLING.** Cambridgeshire. Just off the B1040, about 9½ kilometres (6 miles) east north east of St. Neots.
4. **MAGGIEKNOCKATER.** Grampian. On the A29 about 17½ kilometres (11 miles) south south east of Elgin.
5. **WYRE PIDDLE.** Worcestershire. On the B4084 about 8 kilometres (5 miles) west of Evesham.
6. **WRESSLE.** Just off the A63 about 22½ kilometres (14 miles) south south east of York.
7. **WRANGLE.** Lincolnshire. Half way between Skegness and Boston.
8. **NUTT'S CORNER.** On the A52, 11 kilometres (7 miles) north west of Belfast.
9. **TONGUE.** On the A838 in the extreme north Highlands.
10. **STEWPONEY.** West Midlands. On the A449 about 3 kilometres (2 miles) west of Stourbridge.
11. **SIX MILE BOTTOM.** Cambridgeshire. On the A1304 about 11 kilometres (7 miles) east of Cambridge.
12. **NO PLACE.** Cannot find it on the map but it has 803 inhabitants and they are trying now to get the county to change the name.

Words found on some menus

1. **ANGLAISE.** Garnished with boiled, usually root, vegetables, such as carrots.
2. **AU BEURRE.** With butter. Usually with reference to butter used as a sauce.
3. **AU GRATIN.** Today this is almost always taken to mean baked with cheese on the top but cheese is not an essential ingredient. It can mean 'with bread crumbs sprinkled over the top'.
4. **BÉCHAMEL.** Butter, flour and milk made into a white sauce, which is usually a basis for many flavourings of herbs and so on.
5. **BEURRE NOISETTE.** Butter which is cooked until brown, to which herbs and sometimes lemon are added, to be eaten with fish or meat.
6. **BONNE FEMME.** A mixture of small onions, mushrooms, new potatoes and short strips of bacon.
7. **BOUCHÉE.** This means a mouth-sized portion. Most frequently the word is applied to small vol-au-vents.
8. **BOURGIGNON.** A sauce for red meat made with red wine, usually burgundy, with button mushrooms and small onions.
9. **BRAISÉ.** Meat or vegetable browned in a little fat and cooked in stock, juices, milk or cream.
10. **BROCHETTES.** Meat cooked with herbs on skewers.
11. **BRÛLÉE.** Burnt. Usually applied to burnt sugar as used in caramel dishes.
12. **CANAPÉS.** Small savoury morsels served hot or cold as cocktail snacks, hors d'oeuvres, or end-of-meal savouries. The base is usually biscuit, toast or fried bread.
13. **CHAMPIGNON.** Mushroom or other fungus.
14. **CHARLOTTE.** Pudding of fruit and bread crumbs, baked. It may be in a sponge mixture or with biscuits. There are many varieties of this.
15. **COCK-A-LEEKIE.** Soup made with chicken and leeks.
16. **COLBERT.** A sauce made with Madeira, lemon, meat or fish glaze, butter and light stock.
17. **COLLATION.** Usually a collection of cold food.
18. **COMFITS. (Or CONFITS.)** Small sweetmeats. Sometimes the word is used to mean jam.
19. **CONSOMMÉ.** Strong clear soup.
20. **CRAQUELOTS.** Half bloatered herrings.

21. **CRAWFISH.** A salt water fish looking roughly like a large lobster. Not to be confused (but often is) with next.
22. **CRAYFISH.** A fresh water miniature lobster which was once a great favourite with the Greeks and Romans.
23. **CROMESKIES.** A fritter made by wrapping oysters in paste. Some are made with other fish and even fowl.
24. **CROÛTONS.** Small, usually cubed, pieces of fried bread served with soups.
25. **DUBARRY.** Very glamorous name for simple cauliflowerets coated with mornay sauce and cooked au gratin (see above).
26. **ESCALOPE.** Very thin slice of meat, but usually veal, egged, crumbed and fried.
27. **FANCHETTES.** Small fragile French pastries, baked, filled with cream, topped with meringue and piped with coloured sugar or candied fruit. There are almost as many varieties as there are people who make them.
28. **FILET MIGNON.** Steak cut from the smaller end of a fillet of beef.
29. **FILLET.** Usually the undercut of the sirloin of beef. It can also mean a thick slice of mutton, pork, veal, or boned breast of poultry, or boned fish.
30. **FLAMBÉ.** Literally 'flamed', set alight using brandy.
31. **FLORENTINE.** Another glamorous name meaning served with spinach. (Also an old name for apple pie.)
32. **FOIS GRAS.** The liver of a specially fattened goose. Much cruelty is involved in force-feeding the goose. The delicacy is hard to find. Fortunately.
33. **FONDANTS.** Any sweets that 'melt in the mouth.'
34. **FRICASSÉE.** White meat cut into pieces (rabbit, chicken, turkey, veal, pork, etc.) and cooked again slowly in a flavoured white sauce.
35. **FRIT.** Fried.
36. **GARNI.** Garnished.
37. **GÂTEAU.** Cake. A pretentious word which is better avoided unless applied to a masterpiece, such as Gâteau Mille Feuilles.
38. **HOLLANDAISE.** Dutch style. It usually means an emulsified hot sauce made mainly with butter and egg yolks.
39. **HORS D'OEUVRES.** Savoury titbits before the soup or main course. There should never be so much of it that it impairs the appetite.

40. **HUCKLEBERRY.** Bilberry.
41. **HUMBLES.** The offal of venison. (Sometimes UMBLES.)
    Note: the phrase 'eating humble pie' has its origins here.
    When the lord of the manor dined on venison, the huntsman
    and his men took lower seats and were given the umbles
    made into a pie.
42. **INDIENNE.** Curry-flavoured mayonnaise with chives.
43. **JARDINIÈRE.** This has several meanings all roughly suggesting
    mixed vegetables.
44. **LÉGUMES.** Strictly speaking this means pulse or any plant-
    bearing pods. On a French menu, it usually means
    vegetables in general.
45. **LYONNAISE.** A garnish of fried onions.
46. **MACÉDOINE.** A medley of diced vegetables sometimes
    formed into shapes with gelatine.
47. **À LA MAÎTRE D'HÔTEL.** A method of serving noted for
    simplicity.
48. **MILANAISE.** Mushrooms, shredded ham, tomato sauce with
    pasta.
49. **MINESTRONE.** Italian stew.
50. **MORNAY.** Cheese-flavoured béchamel sauce.
51. **NAPOLITAINE.** Ice cream of several colours and flavours. Also
    a parmesan cheese sauce made with tomatoes. Because of
    the two distinct meanings, take care when ordering it.
52. **NOISETTE.** Best end of neck of lamb, boned and tied into a
    roll, seasoned and chopped into slices.
53. **PITCAITHLY BANNOCK.** Scottish shortbread made with
    almonds, caraway seeds and peel.
54. **PORTUGUESE.** Rich tomato sauce.
55. **PRINCESS.** This word on the menu means that chicken has
    been used.
56. **ROSSINI.** A way of cooking dedicated to the composer of the
    same name. A tournedos (see no. 58 below) rossini consists
    of a fillet steak on top of fried bread, covered with pâté and
    served with a sherry or Madeira sauce spooned over.
57. **SUPRÊME.** As 'Princess' except that only the chicken breasts
    are used.
58. **TOURNEDOS.** An extravagantly cut thick fillet of beef from
    the heart of the fillet. Any word following e.g. ROSSINI,
    denotes the method of cooking.
59. **VALENTINO.** This indicates that asparagus has been used in
    the recipe on the menu.

Bishops' signatures

It may not be well-known outside the church that bishops do not use their names when signing certain documents. Most use their Christian name followed by the town in which they live but there are exceptions. For instance, the Primate of All England whose name without title is Robert Alexander Kennedy Runcie signs himself differently.

1. **ARCHBISHOP AND PRIMATE OF ALL ENGLAND**, Most Reverend and Rt Hon Robert Runcie MC., DD: Robert Cantuar.
2. **BISHOP OF LONDON**, Rt Rev and Rt Hon Graham Leonard DD: Graham Londin (sic).
3. **BISHOP OF WINCHESTER**, Rt Rev John Taylor MA, DD: John Winton.
4. **BISHOP OF CHICHESTER**, Rt Rev Eric Kemp DD: Eric Cicestr. (sic).
5. **BISHOP OF ELY**, Rt Rev Peter Walker DD: Peter Elien.
6. **BISHOP OF EXETER**, Rt Rev Eric Mercer DD: Eric Exon.
7. **BISHOP OF NORWICH**, Rt Rev Maurice Wood DSC., MA: Maurice Norvic.
8. **BISHOP OF OXFORD**, Rt Rev Patrick Rodger: Patrick Oxon.
9. **BISHOP OF PETERBOROUGH**, Rt Rev Douglas Feaver MA: Douglas Petriburg.
10. **BISHOP OF ROCHESTER**, Rt Rev Richard David Say DD: David Roffen.
11. **BISHOP OF EDMUNDSBURY AND IPSWICH**, Rt Rev John Waine BA: John St Edm & Ipswich. (the ampersand is correct here.)
12. **BISHOP OF SALISBURY**, Rt Rev John Baker B. Litt., MA: John Sarum.
13. **BISHOP OF TRURO**, Rt Rev Peter Mumford MA: Peter Truron.
14. **ARCHBISHOP AND PRIMATE OF ENGLAND**, Most Rev and Rt Hon John Habgood: John Ebor. (Not to be confused with the Primate of All England).
15. **BISHOP OF CARLISLE**, Rt Rev Henry David Halsey BA: David Carliol.
16. **BISHOP OF CHESTER**, Rt Rev Michael Baughen BD: Michael Cestr.

Your character from your food

We have all read how palmists say they can read your character from the creases in your palm. Similar strange claims are made about how you wear your shoes out, what you keep on your mantelpiece, what your favourite colour is and so on. All this type of character analysis is verging on the doubtful. But you might like to see what a New York psychiatrist says about the things you eat.

1. A red meat eater is an active go-getter.
2. A vegetable eater is health conscious, high principled, proud and seldom shows anger.
3. A chicken eater is careful with money, cautious and reliable.
4. A dairy produce eater is generous, loyal and extravagant.
5. A sweet and chocolate eater is emotional, high spirited, good company, creative and imaginative.
6. A tinned food eater is liable to act quickly.
7. A frozen food eater is time conscious, unemotional and punctual.

I listed all these types of food, but without the so-called 'characteristics' and showed the list to 100 people near Birmingham's Bull Ring asking them to tick off anything on the list they ate fairly regularly. 93% ticked everything which means that if there is any truth in the psychiatrists claim, 93% of the people are *all* active go-getters, health conscious, high principled, seldom show anger, careful with money, extravagant, generous, loyal, emotional, unemotional, high spirited, imaginative, time conscious, cautious, liable to act quickly and punctual.

Strange facts about some people

1. **Faust**, about whom many stories have been told, including one in which he sold his soul to the devil, was a real person. He was a Doctor of Theology at the University of Wittenberg, Germany, during the 1500s.
2. By the time he was 26 years old, **Napoleon** had conquered Italy.
3. The man who created Sherlock Holmes, **Conan Doyle**, was an ophthalmologist (eye doctor) by profession.

4. **Casanova** was in his time an ecclesiastic, writer, soldier, spy and diplomat. Uncharacteristically, however, he ended his life quietly as a librarian.

5. When **Voltaire's** tomb was opened in 1864, there was no body there, and nobody knows where it is.

6. Explorer, **Sir Richard Burton**, the first Englishman to go to the sacred Moslem city of Mecca, spoke 26 languages and wrote the first English translation of *The Arabian Nights*.

7. The nineteenth century bullfighter, **Lagartijo** (real name Rafael Molina), killed 4,867 bulls, a number never equalled.

8. 'Roll up! Roll up! Come and see the only **blue man** in the world!' That was the side show barker's call at a P. T. Barnum show. The man was indeed blue because by mistake he had permanently dyed himself with silver nitrate.

9. **Napoleon** had a drinking cup made from the skull of Cagliostro the charlatan.

10. **Sir Christopher Wren** was not an architect although he designed (among other things) St Paul's Cathedral. He was an astronomer.

Vegetation which can be used to make wine

1. **Grapes** make the best wine as they have the correct quantities of acid, sugar and tannin. Because the 'bloom' on a grape is yeast, some grape mixes do not need extra yeast.
2. **Rhubarb** wine is the next best but to give it a good flavour add a few dates or raisins before fermenting.
3. **Gooseberry** wine is delightful and was once thought to be a cure for smallpox.
4. **Elderberry** wine is for some reason associated with old aunts.
5. **Banana** wine tastes different from any other wine and it also clears more quickly. Some people use the skins as well which make it turn a muddy grey. The skins are said to improve the flavour, but it is not worth the sacrifice of the golden colour.
6. **Raspberry** wine is made from liquidized raspberries. Unlike many other wines, the resulting fermentation tastes wonderfully of the original fruit.
7. **Dandelion** wine can be very sweet and cloying, not unlike the Italian 'Lacrima Christie' from grapes grown on the slopes of Vesuvius.
8. **Loganberry** wine must be made with relatively few berries because of the high acidity.
9. **Primrose** wine is not to be recommended because it is not worth picking all those beautiful little flowers when the taste is passable but not special.
10. **Cowslip** wine is a great deal of trouble and is not good enough to warrant collecting all those pretty cowslips.
11. **Blackberry** wine is well worth the trouble and tastes like a good burgundy.
12. **Elderflower** wine is totally different from elderberry wine. It makes a delicately flavoured wine, which can be made to sparkle like champagne.

Facts about the Taj Mahal

Some consider this to be the most beautiful building ever and the 8th wonder of the world. It is a mausoleum, built on the south bank of the Jumna river outside Agra in India by the Mogul Emperor Shah Jahan, as a memorial to his wife Arjumand Banu Begum, called Mumtaz Mahal, Chosen One of the Palace. She died in childbirth in 1631. (Some reference books say 1630.)

1. A council of architects from India, Persia and Central Asia prepared plans immediately after her death and building started in 1632. (Some books say 1630.)
2. The accepted plan was the work of a Turk or Persian, called Ustad Isa.
3. The master builders, calligraphers, masons, inlayers and others came from India and Asia.
4. The materials used came from all over India, Europe and Asia.
5. 22,500 workmen were employed daily to complete the building.
6. The building was finished in 1643. It had taken 11 years.
7. The entire Taj complex took another 11 years.
8. The complex measures 1580 m by 304 m (634 yards by 334 yards) aligned north/south.
9. The building is mainly in white marble, carved in open traceries and designs, inlaid with semi-precious stones, many of which have been prised out and stolen.
10. The proportions and balance of the structure with its 4 minarets show Mogul architecture at its finest.
11. The north (river) end contains the most superb design and execution with mosque and *jawab*, 2 symmetrically identical buildings facing the mausoleum itself.
12. On a 7 metre (23 feet) high marble plinth stands the mausoleum itself.
13. The interior of the mausoleum is arranged round an eight-sided room carved with bas relief patterns.
14. The sarcophagi of Begum and Shah Jahan are in a vault below and at ground level. The bodies are in the ones in the vault, the others are presumably a foil to would-be plunderers.

We stopped 100 ladies in London's Oxford Street and asked them what they thought was the most difficult item to iron

PER CENT	ITEM
28 said	SHIRTS
17 said	DENIM JEANS
16 said	TROUSERS
14 said	PLEATS
12 said	FRILLS
11 said	SHEETS

2 said they did not know because they sent their things to the laundry.

Ways to be a wally

Being dubbed a Wally is not a social distinction and has nothing to do with snobbery. Some who should know better can be seen being Wallies on the beaches of the Cote d'Azur, abusing rule 1 below. Some say that thoughtful people are never rude by mistake. A Wally is frequently rude without realising it. But it goes further than insensitive behaviour and mere vulgarity. To find out how to be a Wally, now read on . . .

1. Wear socks with sandals.
2. Put a foreign country's plate on your car, such as F for France, when your car was registered in England.
3. Be rude to restaurant staff whom you know cannot reply.
4. Have any stickers on your rear windscreen, especially one on a Mini that reads 'When I grow up I shall be a Rolls Royce'.
5. Smother your food in strong sauce.
6. Smoke in a non-smoking house.
7. Go to a party and later don't bother to ring and say thank you.
8. Have your vest showing under your shirt.
9. Only laugh at a rich man's jokes.
10. Wave at television cameras.
11. Read magazines only and no books.
12. Blame the system for your failures.
13. Sink your individuality by imitating someone else, e.g. girls who copy hair styles of film stars and princesses; boys who like to look like Elvis. No reports of them looking like Boy George yet.
14. Drink lager. Girls may drink lager but are Wallies if they drink port and lemon.
15. Wear a T shirt printed with something such as 'I LOVE PARIS'.
16. Wear very long shorts.
17. Fit your car with a multitone hooter and hang toys from the interior rearview mirror.
18. Play a radio out of doors where others hear it.
19. Drink beer until your stomach hangs over the front of your trousers.
20. Supply the punch line to other people's jokes.

Simpson's-in-the-Strand (London) menu

The General Manager of this noted restaurant, M.C. Williams, kindly sent me some of the costs of my favourite lunch there over the years. Even his painstaking research could not unearth all the prices which are lost in the mists of antiquity. Perhaps a reader, going through great grandfather's old suits, might be able to supply the missing costs.

DISH	1913	1930	1940	1950	1960	1970	1980	1984
TROUT	—	—	—	10p	20p	55p	£2.00	£2.45
SADDLE OF LAMB	12½p	20p	20p	27½p	37½p	72½p	£5.50.	£6.45
VEGETABLE	3¾p	3½p	6p	8½p	15p	22½p	65p	85p
MUSHROOMS ON TOAST	5p	7½p	6p	10p	17½p	25p	90p	£1.15
CARAFE OF CLARET	—	—	—	62½p	60p	£1.00	£4.60	£5.65

Things you could buy for an old penny

Before decimal currency, which was introduced on February 15, 1971, there were 240d or pence for £1.00, today there are 100. This means that the new penny is worth 2.4 old pennies. Keep that in mind as you read this list.

There was a time (in the 1920s) when for 1d you could buy:
1. A newspaper.
2. A stamp for a postcard.
3. A platform ticket.
4. 2 bags of sherbert with a tube of licorice to suck it through.
5. A comic.
6. A sugar mouse.
7. A box of matches.
8. You could weigh yourself.
9. 2 bangers for Guy Fawkes night.
10. A pair of boot laces.
11. Bag of nails from the ironmonger.
12. And even further back MARKS & SPENCER'S slogan was:
    'DON'T ASK THE PRICE — IT'S A PENNY.'

Twelve signs of the Zodiac

In order, with the legends of how they arrived in the heavens. The dates when the sun enters and leaves a sign can vary by plus or minus one day.

These first six are the northern summer signs.

1. **ARIES** March 21 to April 20. The sun is in this sign during and between those dates. From the legend that the RAM with the golden fleece, which carried on its back Phrixus and Helle, was sacrificed to Zeus, who set it as a constellation in the sky. Some say it was the ram which guided Dionysus to water in the Libyan desert.

2. **TAURUS** April 21 to May 20. The BULL in heaven. Legend says it is either the one in whose shape Zeus wooed Europa, or the one loved by Pasiphae, which was caught by Hercules, brought to Greece and killed by Theseus at Marathon.

3. **GEMINI** May 21 to June 20. The TWINS in heaven. Legend says they are either the twin sons of the Theban Antiope, Ampihion and Zethus, or they are Castor and Polydeuces (Pollux). It has also been said that they are Hercules and Apollo, or that they are Triptolemus and Iasion, respectively pupil and lover of Demeter, or the Great Gods of Samothrace.

4. **CANCER** June 21 to July 23. The CRAB constellation appears when the sun has reached its highest northern limit and starts to go back to the south. Its return is sideways — like a crab. Legend says it is the creature sent to attack Hercules, when he went to chop off the heads of the Hydra. It grabbed his foot in a claw but he killed it and Juno took it to heaven.

5. **LEO** July 23 to August 21. The LION constellation. Legend says this is the lion killed and skinned by Hercules.

6. **VIRGO** August 22 to September 21. This is the sign of the VIRGIN, the Starry Maid. Legend sometimes has it she was Astraea, identified with Justice who left the earth for the heavens when men became too wicked to associate with.

Other stories identify her with one of the better known goddesses, such as Demeter, Core, or a foreign deity, such as Isis or Atargatis.

The next six are the southern winter signs.

7. **LIBRA** September 22 to October 22. This is the name of an ancient constellation. It means the SCALES or BALANCE because if the day were to be weighed with the night they would be found to be equal.

8. **SCORPIO** October 23 to November 22. This sign should more correctly be called Scorpius or Nepa in Latin. Legend has it that Orion had boasted that he could kill any creature. A SCORPION was sent as a punishment for his bravado, which stung and killed him. For this, Jupiter raised the scorpion to heaven. Legend also has it that the scorpion carries an oil to act as an antidote to its own poison.

9. **SAGITTARIUS** November 23 to December 21. This translates comfortably into the ARCHER or ARROW BEARER, but in legend it is a CENTAUR, a beast, half horse and half man, which lived in old Thessaly. It is possible that the origin of this can be found in the expert horsemanship of the real inhabitants. Chiron was the mythical centaur who taught Achilles and others, music, archery and medicine. Jupiter put Chiron into the heavens.

10. **CAPRICORN** December 22 to January 20. The legend has it that Pan, terrified of Typhon (a monster with 100 heads) changed himself into a GOAT. Jupiter then made him into one of the signs of the Zodiac.

11. **AQUARIUS** January 21 to February 18. The legend has it that the WATERBEARER was Ganymede, son of king Laomedon of Troy. Because of his great beauty the gods carried him off to Mount Olympus, where he became cupbearer to Zeus. Olympus is a mountain on the border of Macedonia and Thessaly. Being the highest peak in Greece, it was considered in mythology to be the home of the gods.

12. PISCES February 19 to March 20. There are many associations of these two FISHES with their tails tied together, although some paintings show them as linked by a thread from their mouths. Legend has it that Aphrodite and Eros jumped into a river to escape the 100-headed Typhon (see Capricorn) and they turned into fishes.

Seven champagne bottle sizes

1. **MAGNUM**   55 ounces
2. **JEROBOAM**   108 ounces
3. **REHODOAM**   163 ounces
4. **METHUSELAH**   216.4 ounces
5. **SALMANAZAR**   324.5 ounces
6. **BALTHAZAR**   432.7 ounces
7. **NEBUCHADNEZZAR**   541 ounces

These terms are also applied by some to sizes of bottles of other wines.

Horrible happenings of 100 years ago (1884)

1. **JANUARY.** A railway bridge falls down between Preston and Wigan injuring many and killing 7 people.
2. **FEBRUARY.** Someone tries to blow up Victoria Station with serious consequences. Presumably the same person or people also try to blow up Charing Cross Station and Paddington Station. The explosive is discovered before it goes off.
3. **MARCH.** Nothing very dreadful happens except that a clerk is mysteriously murdered and no one finds out who did it.
4. **APRIL.** There is a terrible earthquake in Essex that lasts about half a minute, some buildings fall down.
5. **MAY.** Two damaging dynamite explosions in London. One at Scotland Yard and the other in St James's Square.
6. **JUNE.** The Theatre Royal, Edinburgh is gutted by fire. Religious cranks say it is an 'act of God' because of the immorality of theatres.
7. **JULY.** A railway accident at Penistone killing 19 and injuring 30.
8. **AUGUST.** Those people with dynamite are at it again, this time trying to blow up the Post Office at Nottingham.

9. **SEPTEMBER.** Captain Dudley and 2 others, survivors of the wrecked yacht 'Mignonette', confess to having eaten one crew member, Richard Parker, and are charged with this offence.
10. **OCTOBER.** Half of Moscow burns down.
11. **NOVEMBER.** Someone shouts 'Fire!' in the Star Theatre at Glasgow. The audience panic trying to escape and many are crushed.
12. **DECEMBER.** The people of Sheffield take a dislike to Mormons and riot against them. These people with dynamite turn up again but are unsuccessful in their attempt at blowing up London Bridge.

Haggis ingredients

A 2 hour boiled haggis will keep for 2 weeks because it becomes very hard. If you add onion it will not keep as long. This is what can be in it. For cooking instructions look it up in any good cookbook.

1 calf's udder. 1 calf's kidney. 1 calf's pluck. 1 bay leaf. 12 sprigs of parsley. 1 handful of young green onions. 1 handful of shallots. 1 handful of small mushrooms. A tablespoonful of butter. Wineglass of Madeira wine. Salt and pepper. Web of veal fat. 2 tablespoons of gravy. 2 egg yolks. 1 handful of brown bread crumbs. A glass of whisky.

Do not forget that if you want to keep it a while, leave out the onion. Cook for a couple of hours in the stomach of a sheep. Prick it well or it will explode in the boiling water and blow up your kitchen.

Do not add the whisky to the haggis. Drink it slowly while you get on with the work. It is a great help.

A parcel of haggis was flown to Brazil in 1965. After examining it, customs officers said it could not properly be defined. It was analysed and declared to be a fertilizer.

Information about Halley's Comet

The comet is on its way back. You will see it clearly, and it will be more interesting if you know something about it.

1. In January 1986 you will see what appears as a new star. It will not be very bright: it will look about average.
2. It was furthest away from us in 1948 when it started its return journey. Speed: about 2,100 miles an hour and accelerating. Distance: about 3,300,000,000 miles from the Sun.
3. In 1983 it must have looked quite good from Saturn as it passed by, but you would not have seen it as it was still about 900,000,000 miles away from the Earth.
4. If you see it through a telescope at the beginning of 1985 it will be passing Jupiter and will be about 480,000,000 miles away from you.
5. Sales of telescopes and binoculars will rise as press coverage increases and everyone will want to look at this shining, spinning, 4-mile diameter object which is really a mass of solar system dust made up of many elements frozen in ammonia, carbon monoxide and water.
6. As it nears the Sun, it comes to the boil from the heat and hides itself under a veil called the *coma*. From the Sun emanates solar wind, which sweeps most of the veil back to become the familiar 'tail', which might stretch as far as 70,000,000 miles. It is now moving at almost 105,000 miles an hour and still accelerating.
7. Its violent swing round the Sun will be sometime about February 8, 9 and 10, 1986, at a speed which will hurl it back to the outer limits of our Solar System. Now the solar winds will push the tail out at an angle and subsequently almost in front of the comet. Gradually it will fade from our sight to prepare itself for another 76 year journey. It will not reappear until about the year 2062.
8. In April 1986, if all calculations are correct, it will be closest to the Earth, dominating the night sky and visible in the day time as well.
9. Five space craft will be sent to meet it. Europe is sending one, the Japanese two and the Russians two. Our space machine will hurtle through the tail at over 150,000 miles an hour taking photographs and samples of the tail. It is hoped that,

because most of this comet is frozen, it will be possible to find out from samples just what was the origin of our solar system.

10. Those of you who are superstitious may see this visitation as an omen of evil. This kind of rubbish is without foundation. Certainly you will read of its appearance at the Battle of Hastings when Harold was killed. That was bad luck for him. But it was good luck for William who is reported to have said 'A new star. A new king.'

Facts about the world's most venomous snake

1. It is called parademanisa microlepidotus and nicknamed PM for short. PM also stands for Post Mortem.
2. It lives in central Australia.
3. Fully grown it seldom exceeds 2 metres (6 ft).
4. It is brown and matches the earth it slides on.
5. It is about 300 times more poisonous than the rattlesnake.
6. It is about 20 times more poisonous than the cobra.
7. It was not examined under laboratory conditions until 1975.
8. One bite will usually inject you with about 50 milligrams of venom.
9. Scientists have produced an antidote which will save your life — if you can get it quickly enough.

A list of money terms which often confuse

Here is just a small collection of the words which make up the language of the business of money. It deliberately leaves out obvious expressions such as 'debit' and 'credit'. This list has been compiled with the generous help of Paul Legg of *Barclay's Bank Trust Company Limited*.

1. **AVERAGE** A payment made by the insurance company of less than the value because of under insurance.
2. **BEAR** One who sells what he does not hold in the hope that he can buy it for less before settling.
3. **BLUE CHIP** Ordinary shares of the highest investment calibre.
4. **BULL** One who buys in order to wait and sell for a profit when the shares have risen in value. (Compare this with BEAR.)

5. **CASH FLOW** The amount by which a company's liquid resources are increased during the year.
6. **COLLATERAL** Security for a loan.
7. **CUM** A prefix meaning 'with', thus *cum dividend* means with dividend and *cum bonus* means with bonus.

8. **DAYS OF GRACE** Time allowed by most insurance companies still covering the insured although he may not have paid his insurance on the day stated on the contract.

9. **DEAR MONEY** Money on which the rate of interest payable is higher than average.

10. **DEBENTURE** A paper showing that a company has borrowed money from someone. That person being a **debenture** holder will receive his interest before a shareholder.

11. **EQUITIES** Shares having a claim to participate in the profits of a company after it has satisfied all charges and met any preferential dividends.

12. **FINANCE COMPANY** Money lender.

13. **FRANKED INCOME** Income received by one company from another whose profits have already borne Corporation Tax.

14. **FUTURES** Anything bought and sold for delivery at a future date.

15. **GILT-EDGED SECURITY** Stock of the highest quality, usually Government stocks.

16. **HOT MONEY** International movements of short-term capital, generally of a speculative nature in anticipation of a currency devaluation or appreciation.

17. **LIMITED COMPANY** More properly *Limited liability company* because the owners, in the event of money being lost, do not by law have to pay out more than the nominal value of the shares held. Hence the words **limited liability**.

18. **OPEN ENDED FUND** Term applied to a Unit Trust whereby its capital fluctuates according to the amount invested.

19. **PORTFOLIO** Shares held by one owner who can be a person or an institution.

20. **PREFERENCE SHARES** Shares on which interest must be paid before any others, hence the word **preference**. Owners of such shares have first right to repayment of capital in the event of the company being wound up.

21. **PUISNE** A legal mortgage without the relative Title Deeds.

22. **SCRIP ISSUE** If a company holds too much in reserve, the chairman cannot go out and spend it himself (however much he feels like it). As the company is owned by the shareholders, the reserve is issued in the form of shares, known as 'scrip issue', which are dealt out to those already holding shares.

23. **SINKING FUND** A fund established to extinguish a liability, usually by making regular payments over a period.

24. **STAG** A speculator on the Stock Exchange who subscribes to a new issue of shares in the hope of selling them for a quick profit.
25. **THIRD PARTY INSURANCE** Insurance against claims from someone outside the agreement. For example if you run your car through a shop window, your third party insurance will pay for the damage to the shop.

Regretted statements

1. **H.G. WELLS**, author of many books including 'The First Men on the Moon.' He wrote 'I do not think it probable that aeronautics will ever come into play as a serious modification of transport . . .'
2. **SIR HAROLD SPENCER JONES**, Astronomer Royal from 1933-55, said that space travel would never be possible as nothing could escape the Earth's gravitational field.
3. **H.G. WELLS**, (again) said that a submarine would never amount to anything except as a container to suffocate its crew.
4. **BISHOP WRIGHT**, father of Wilbur and Orville Wright, 'Men will never fly because flying is reserved for the angels.'
5. **ALEXANDER DOW**, the president of the Detroit Edison Co wanted to talk Ford out of 'messing about with petrol engines, because soon everything will be electric.' (Perhaps in 100 years he will be right.)
6. **THOMAS EDISON**, one of the greatest inventors of his day, in 1926 said publicly that the people would never bother to support radio. (*The British Broadcasting Company*, as it was then, started broadcasting in 1922.)
7. **FRANKLIN D. ROOSEVELT**, in 1922 said aeroplanes would be useful mainly for reconnaissance as they would always lack the range and capacity for a bomb which could sink a battleship.
8. **SIR HUMPHREY DAVY** said in 1812, knowing a company had been formed for street gas lighting in 1808, 'It would be just as easy to bring down a bit of the moon to light London.'

Eight reasons to eat garlic

1. **BOLIVIAN BULL FIGHTERS** SAY THE SMELL INTIMIDATES THE BULL.
2. **SOLDIERS OF ANCIENT ROME** WOULD CHEW A WHOLE CLOVE BEFORE BATTLE CONVINCED IT GAVE THEM COURAGE.
3. **ITALIAN SINGERS** SAY IT IMPROVES THE VOICE.
4. **IN THE MIDDLE AGES** IT WAS THOUGHT TO BE A CURE FOR WHOOPING COUGH.
5. **CRUSHED, MIXED WITH GOOSE GREASE** AND RUBBED INTO THE SOLES OF THE FEET, IT WAS THOUGHT TO BE A CURE FOR A SORE THROAT.
6. **A PROFESSOR** FROM WEST GERMANY SAYS IT CLEARS THE FATTY BUILD-UP IN THE BLOOD VESSELS AND SO PREVENTS HEART ATTACKS.
7. **20 PEOPLE IN 100** THINK IT KEEPS INFLUENZA GERMS AWAY. (Could be that germs have a sense of smell?)
8. **IT KEEPS VAMPIRES**, SUCH AS DRACULA, AWAY.

Paired words that sound wrong when reversed

1. MASH AND SAUSAGES.
2. SWIM OR SINK.
3. CONS AND PROS.
4. FRO AND TO.
5. A SENSE OF WRONG AND RIGHT.
6. ROLL AND ROCK.
7. BUTTER AND BREAD.
8. A MATTER OF DEATH OR LIFE.
9. ORDER AND LAW.
10. SWINGING FORTH AND BACK.
11. DOWN AND UP.
12. KIDNEY AND STEAK.
13. CREAM AND STRAWBERRIES.
14. WHITE AND BLACK TV SET.
15. SQUEAK AND BUBBLE.
16. SAUCER AND CUP.
17. WIFE AND MAN.

A list of Chinese interest

At some time or other, all these things have happened or still happen in China.

1. The family name comes first. After that comes the individual intimate name, e.g. Brown John.
2. A Chinese person would see a great deal of sense if we addressed our letters so: England, Warwickshire, Birmingham, Edgbaston, South Road, Number 22, Flat C, Brown, John. The more you think about that the more sense it makes. At least the postal authorities would be able to read the envelope from the top to bottom, instead of bottom to top.
3. When the Chinese teacup has a saucer it is put on the top and not underneath. How, asks the Chinese housewife, is the tea kept warm with this crazy western idea of putting the saucer under the teacup?

4. When one Chinese friend meets another they do not shake each other's hands but they shake their own. How sensible! They cannot catch any germs from each other that way.

5. Getting out of a hot bath the Chinese person will dry with a cold wet towel. Very refreshing. Very stimulating.

6. Why let the labourer get wet building a house from the bottom up? How much more logical to put up the outer supports and build a roof first, then build the house. Those westerners let each floor suffer with rain as they build up to the roof. Start with roof and house and builder are happy.

7. Chinese compass points south. No logic, but then no logic in western compass pointing north.

8. Why do westerners say that the earliest attempts at gas lighting started in Europe in 1786, when Chinese have used gas for lighting and cooking thousands of years BC, brought up through bamboo pipes from beds of rock salt?

9. Westerner gets into hot bath which slowly goes cold. Chinese has much more sense. He lights a small flame under the bath and gets into warm water which gets slowly warmer. Flame too small to boil occupant on bath night.

10. Chinese doctor cannot draw fee from sick patient. When patient better doctor get money. Very sensible idea.

If you are superstitious do not read this unlucky thirteen list

There is no way of telling why 13 and Fridays are unlucky to those naive enough to be superstitious, but here is a list of unfortunate associations and people's reactions.

1. Cain killed Abel on a Friday.
2. At a banquet in Valhalla, Loki who was unasked, sat down and made the number up to 13. Balder was killed. Now Norse superstition claims that the 13th guest at a banquet is the spirit of evil.
3. There were 13 at the Last Supper when Christ sat down with his 12.
4. It has often proved unlucky for a ship to sail on a Friday especially if it is the 13th.
5. Adam and Eve ate the forbidden fruit on a Friday.
6. Adam and Eve died on a Friday.
7. Some hotels have no rooms numbered 13.
8. Some streets and flats are numbered 12a rather than have their real number, 13, acknowledged.
9. Buddhists and Brahmins consider Friday the worst of days.

10. Friday was the day for hanging criminals, and was once known as 'Hanging Day'.
11. He who laughs on a Friday will weep on Sunday. (Racine '*Les Plaideurs*').
12. An old saying has it 'A Friday moon brings foul weather.'
13. Christ was crucified on a Friday.

Twelve famous last words

1. 'Now comes the mystery'. **HENRY WARD BEECHER**, American Congregationalist preacher, 1837.
2. 'I have been a most unconscionable time dying, but I hope you will excuse it.' **CHARLES II**, 1685.
3. 'Be sure you show that mob my head. It will be a long time before they see its like.' **GEORGES DANTON**, one of the greatest figures in the French Revolution. To the executioner in 1794.
4. 'All my possessions for a moment of time.' **ELIZABETH I**, Queen of England, 1603.
5. 'Wonderful! Wonderful, this death!' **WILLIAM ETTY**, considered at one time to be the greatest English figure painter, 1849.
6. 'If Mr Selwyn calls, let him in. If I am alive I shall be very glad to see him, and if I am dead he will be very glad to see me.' **LORD HENRY HOLLAND**, Liberal statesman, nephew of Charles James Fox, 1840.
7. 'There are 6 guineas for you and do not hack me as you did my Lord Russell.' **DUKE OF MONMOUTH**, beheaded on Tower Hill, to his executioner on July 15, 1685.
8. 'See me safe up. For my coming down, let me shift for myself.' **SIR THOMAS MORE**, English statesman, as he ascended the scaffold on July 7, 1535.
9. 'Die? My dear doctor, that is the last thing I shall do!' **VISCOUNT HENRY PALMERSTON**, British Prime Minister, 1865.
10. 'What an artist the world is losing in me.' **NERO**, immensely vain and debauched Roman Emperor, 68.
11. 'I am going to seek the great perhaps.' **FRANCOIS RABELAIS**, French satirist to whom France owes the melon, artichoke, and carnation, 1553 or 4.
12. 'I'll be shot if I don't believe I'm dying.' **LORD THURLOW**, politician, a vulgar, arrogant, profane and immoral man.

A list of ten languages

Living in an English speaking country and knowing it is spoken in vast countries, such as Canada, USA, Australia, and so on gives us the idea that English is the most spoken language in the world. Here are the first ten most popular languages with a rough idea of how many people speak them.

LANGUAGE	AREA SPOKEN	NUMBER WHO SPEAK IT
1. MANDARIN CHINESE	N & E Central China	580,000,000
2. ENGLISH	British Isles, N. America, Commonwealth, S. Africa, and many other places.	355,000,000
3. HINDI	Parts of India.	170,000,000
4. RUSSIAN	Russia and penetrating into satellite countries.	165,000,000
5. SPANISH	Spain and part of S. America.	140,000,000
6. GERMAN	Germany, Switzerland, Austria.	110,000,000
7. JAPANESE	Japan.	100,000,000
8. BENGALI	Parts of India, Bangladesh.	95,000,000
9. FRENCH	France, N. Africa, Canada, Switzerland.	80,000,000
10. PORTUGUESE	Portugal, old Portuguese colonies, Brazil.	75,000,000

The nine muses

In ancient Greek religion these were a group of goddesses of obscure origin who centred on Mount Helicon in Boeotia. Confusion about them abounds. For instance they are referred to as virgins and yet they bore children. Taking them in alphabetical order this is what they represented:

1. **CALLIOPE.** Patron of epic poetry.
2. **CLIO.** Patron of history and scrolls.
3. **ERATO.** Patron of lyrical and erotic poetry.
4. **EUTERPE.** Patron of flutes and tragedy.
5. **MELPOMENE.** Patron of the lyre and tragedy.
6. **POLYMNIA.** Patron of geometry and dancing.
7. **TERPSICHORE.** Patron of lyric poetry and dancing.
8. **THALIA.** Patron of comedy.
9. **URANIA.** Patron of astronomy.

100 people named dogs they fear most

55 said	**ALSATIAN** (German Shepherd)
15 said	**DOBERMAN PINSCHER**
10 said	**BULLDOG**
6 said	**IRISH WOLFHOUND**
4 said	**POODLE**

The missing ten percent were a mixture of 'none', 'all' and 'don't know.'

Occult beliefs

NAME	DIVINATION METHOD
1. ALEXTOROMANTIA.	Observation of direction taken by a cock or hen released in the middle of a circle.
2. ALEXTRYOMANCY.	Reading the random patterns made by scattering grain.
3. AMNIOMANCY.	Revealing a baby's future from the arrangement of the amniotic membrane at the child's birth.
4. ARITHMOMANCY.	Abstruse numerical calculations.
5. BELOMANCY.	Flight patterns and landing of arrows shot at random.
6. CEREOSCOPY.	Dropping hot wax on to cold water.
7. CLEDONISM.	Omens in first words heard in the morning.
8. HARUSPICY.	Deducing the will of the gods from the appearance of the entrails of a sacrificed animal.
9. HYDROSCOPY.	Reading ripples created by throwing three pebbles into a pool.

10.	KIEIDISCOPY.	Swinging of a key or small object on a string.
11.	METOPOSCOPY.	Reading from the markings on a person's face or forehead.
12.	ORNITHOMANCY.	Reading flight patterns of birds.
13.	PYROMANCY.	Reading movement of flames.
14.	RHABDOMANCY.	Using a bent hazel stick as an indicator of gold, water, etc.
15.	SCAPULOMANCY.	Reading cracks in roasted shoulder bones of sheep.
16.	SCREEOLOGY.	Looking into crystal balls.

A list for migraine sufferers

Some doctors say that some migraine sufferers might do better to avoid some of the following. That cautiously worded sentence shows that people vary. No two are the same, and different things set off migraine in different people.

1. Strobing or flickering light, such as a neon lamp about to fail, or a car journey down an avenue of trees when the sun is near the horizon.
2. Going out on a very cold day.
3. Wheat.
4. Cheese.
5. Beef.
6. Oranges.
7. Red wine.
8. Eggs.
9. Tea.
10. Coffee.
11. Chocolate.
12. 3-D films for which spectacles have to be worn.
13. Fluid retention.
14. Noise.

A list of parlour games great-grandmother played

In the days before television and radio many people would spend the evening playing the piano, singing and playing games. The following were all popular during the early part of the reign of Queen Victoria (1837-1901).

1. **THE BELLMAN.** This is a version of Blind Man's Buff. One of the company is chosen to carry a small bell, the rest of the company, but not the bellman, are all blindfolded. The bellman must ring his bell from time to time and the blind man who catches him changes places with him.

2. **MUSICAL POTATOES.** The company sit on the floor and one person sits at the piano to supply the music. Potatoes are issued to all but one of those on the floor. The music starts and the potatoes are passed behind their backs to the left from one to another. When the music stops, the player without a potato is out of the game. A potato is taken away and so on until the last one is declared the winner.

3. **HOT BOILED BEANS.** One of the company leaves the room while a walnut is hidden. When that person returns the others all sing 'Hot boiled beans and bacon for supper, hurry up before it gets cold!' The object is for the solo player to find the walnut. He is allowed clues which he finds by asking 'Am I warm?' If the reply is 'cold' he knows he is in the wrong part of the room.

4. **THE OBJECT GAME.** This is the possible origin of today's familiar **Twenty Questions**. The company of, say, 12 people divide into two teams of 6. One member of each team leaves the room and the two teams of 5 go to opposite ends of the room, so neither team can hear what the others are saying. Each team decides on an object to be guessed. The two outside return to their respective teams and by asking questions which can be answered only by YES or NO they have to guess what the object is.

5. **SHADOWS.** This needs a large room. A white sheet is stretched as firmly as possible across the middle of the room. If it is a party of 10, 5 go one side and 5 the other. There is an oil lamp at one end of the room so that anyone crossing the sheet will throw a shadow on it. It is up to the company on the other side to guess whose shadow it is. Hunched shoulders, false noses, and cardboard profiles are all part of the fun to put the other team off.

6. **POOR KITTY.** The object of this game is not to smile. The first to do so either pays a forfeit or is out. Everyone except 'Kitty' sits on the floor in a circle. Whoever plays Kitty must walk on all fours round the inside of the circle and stop from time to time in front of a player to say 'Miaow!'. The player must keep a straight face and say 'Poor Kitty!' Kitty goes on round and the next person confronted with Kitty is miaowed at twice, and twice says 'Poor Kitty!'. The next person confronted is miaowed at 3 times and 'Poor Kitty!' is repeated 3 times. So it goes on, but not for long because soon everyone laughs.

7. **THIS IS MY NOSE.** A player touches his ear and says 'This is my nose.' The next player must touch his *nose* and say it is some other part of his body, for instance as he touches his nose he

says 'This is my foot.' The next must touch his foot and say something like 'This is my chin.' It is not long before a player touches (say) his elbow and says 'This is my elbow.' When this happens he is out.

8. **CRAMBO.** This was at one time the most popular 'parlour' game in the British Isles. One member of the party leaves the room while the rest of the company decide on a word such as 'Pool'. On the return of the one outside, a clue is given him such as 'Rule'. He then knows the word must rhyme with 'Rule'. The questions and answers are devious. He asks 'Is it an idiot?' Answer 'No it is not a Fool.' And so the game progresses until the victim gets the correct word. The scoring is simple. Five seconds are allowed for the question and five seconds for the answer. If the solo player cannot ask a question within five seconds he has 10 points added to his score and he is out. One person notes the number of questions needed to arrive at the answer. Each one of the company plays and the one with the lowest score at the end of the round is the winner.

9. **GHOSTS.** The object of this game is to take it in turns to spell a word, he who finishes it is penalized. For example: Player 1. A. Player 2. P. Player 3. P. Player 4. L. If player 5 says E, he has finished the word APPLE, but if he has the wit to say A he is still in the game. If challenged as to what the word might be he will say APPLAUSE. The challenger loses a 'life' and the game goes on.

10. **WANDERER'S ALPHABET.** The company sit in a ring and one begins by saying 'I am going to Birmingham.' He addresses the player on his right with the question 'And where might you be going?' That player must then claim to be going to a place which starts with the letter ending the last place. He replies 'I am going to Morocco,' and turning to the player on his right asks 'And where might you be going?' The game goes on and anyone not replying in three seconds is out. By elimination a winner is found.

Camel facts

Camels have a most superior look and when you have read this list you will see that, although they do not mean to look quite so snobby, it is quite justified.

1. There are no wild camels. They are all owned.
2. A camel carries a 193 kg (425 pound) burden with ease.
3. A camel can walk 38 km (24 miles) a day with a load and with ease.
4. Temperatures of 54°C (130°F) or higher do not worry it.
5. It can walk in great heat for five days without water.
6. When it is thirsty it will drink up to 118 litres (26 gallons).
7. It will munch merrily away on desert scrub from which it gains nourishment.
8. The hump or humps (1 on the dromedary, 2 on the bactrian) can each hold 27 kg (60 pounds) of fat which is capable of producing water when needed, although most water is stored in the stomach.
9. Wind, heat and sand are all kept at bay by the camel's brown or grey fur coat.
10. It can project its eyebrows to keep the sun out of its eyes.
11. It can keep the sand out of its eyes with its triple eyelids.
12. It can keep the sand out of its nose by closing its nostrils.
13. It has flat pads for feet which is why it does not sink into the sand.
14. Its milk is richer than cows' milk.
15. Camel flesh properly cooked is delicious. The beast is too useful to be slaughtered for meat but it was once a valued dish.
16. Camels' wool makes excellent blankets.
17. Camel leather makes gloves, shoes, handbags and suitcases.
18. Camel bone is often passed off as ivory when carved.
19. Strange though it may seem, desert nights are very cold but a good fire can be made from camel dung.
20. Camels are kind and will not bite or throw up at you unless their owner has ill-treated them.

Hiccup cures

There are many cures for hiccups but it is impossible to verify any of them, because (with the exception of the occasions when this curious behaviour is a serious illness) hiccups stop of their own accord. Here is a list of so-called cures:

1. Put a sheet of brown paper on your chest next to your skin.
2. Eat a banana.
3. Drink a glass of water from the side of the glass furthest from your chest.
4. Eat a tablespoon of brown sugar.
5. Get someone to give you a fright.
6. Breathe in and out of a paper bag.
7. Drink a glass of lemonade in very small sips following each sip with a swallow and each swallow with a swallow before taking the next sip.
8. Stand on your head.
9. Drop a cold key down your back.
10. Drink a tablespoon of vinegar.

A list of fallacies

1. **Aesop did not write fables.** (See also page 70.) If he existed, which is doubtful, he may have been a Phrygian slave during the 6th century BC. Some of the fables credited to him were written on Egyptian papyri during the 16th century BC. An Italian named Babrisus collected most of these fables together in about 230 AD.

2. **The pub sign, 'The Bag o' Nails', has nothing to do with bags or nails.** It is a colloquialism for 'The Bacchanals' from *Bacchanalia*, the Latin term for the orgiastic rites of Bacchus.

3. **Barbarians were not cruel and crude.** Many think this is an insulting term but it comes from the sounds *ba-ba-ba*, which is what the Greeks thought those who did not speak Greek were saying. Barbarians were as civilized as any but did not speak Greek.

4. **You have never had a pencil with lead in it.** If you found one you would be hard put to make it write. The black stuff in a 'lead' pencil is plumbago or graphite, a form of carbon. Other black substances are also used, but not lead.

5. **Julius Caesar was never a Roman Emperor.** He was consul five times. He was a dictator; but there was no Roman Empire until after he died.

6. **Guinea pigs do not come from Guinea.** They come from Peru.

7. **Lemmings do not march off in armies and commit suicide.** Every now and then these little creatures increase their population to such an extent that they have to leave their safe pastures and look for new ones. In so doing they swim rivers, lakes and pools arriving safely on the other bank to find fresh food. However, they cannot distinguish between a river and the sea. Some of them try to swim across the sea and find out too late that it is too big and they are too far out.

8. **Nero did not fiddle while Rome burned.** There were no fiddles until sometime in the 1500s. Nor was he at the

spectacle strumming his lyre and singing. The burning of Rome had nothing to do with him, as he was at his villa at Antrium 80 kilometres (50 miles) away at the time.

9. **Lightning strikes in the same place frequently.** A church on the top of a hill with a lightning conductor will be struck frequently, but harmlessly.

10. **The pantomime Cinderella should not have glass slippers.** This is the result of a mistake in translation. The original story said the slippers were 'pantoufles en vair' which means 'slippers of ermine'. The word 'vair' sounds very like 'verre' meaning glass. And that is how the pantomime producer's headache of finding glass slippers started.

A list of radio comedy greats

This list has been compiled by Bobby Jaye, Head of Light Entertainment BBC Radio with one of the top producers in the same department, Richard Edis. The detailed research and the supplying of the names of artists, writers and dates is the work of Marc Platt and others in the BBC Programme Index department.

I.T.M.A. Probably the first 'great' radio programme was I.T.M.A. (It's That Man Again) which started on July 12 1939, and set a new style of radio show.

   The last broadcast of that remarkable series was on January 6, 1949. In the cast of that last one were Tommy Handley (who died two days later), Jack (I don't mind if I do, sir) Train, Hugh Morton, Fred Yule, Diana Morrison, Deryck Guyler, Joan (It's being so cheerful that keeps me going) Harben and Hattie Jacques. With them were Handley's Kerbside Choristers directed by George Mitchell, the Augmented BBC Variety Orchestra was conducted by Rae Jenkins, the script was by Ted Kavanagh and the show was produced by Francis Worsley. Dolly (Can I do you now, sir?) Summers had left the cast some time before the last show to try her luck on her own.

BAND WAGGON's first broadcast was on January 5, 1938, the last was on December 2, 1939. The run was relatively short but the impact was terrific. The cast of a revival for the Jubilee on November 13, 1947, was Arthur Askey and Richard Murdoch with Miff Ferrie's Jakdauz, who were Miff Ferrie, George Crow and Terry Brown. The rest of the billing reads Bettie Bucknelle, Bill Emmings, Fred Yule, The Bandwaggoners conducted by Phil Cardew, at the organ, Charles Smart. The production was by Harry S. Pepper and Gordon Crier.

TAKE IT FROM HERE ran from December 7, 1943, to March 3, 1960 with interruptions. The cast of the first was Joy Nichols, Dick Bentley, Jimmy Edwards, Wilfred Babbage and the Keynotes. The Augmented BBC Revue Orchestra was conducted by Frank Cantell. The script was by Frank Muir and Denis Norden. The show was produced by Charles Maxwell.

By 1954 Dick Bentley and Jimmy Edwards had been joined by Wallas Eaton, Alma Cogan and June Whitfield.

MUCH BINDING IN THE MARSH had its first airing on January 2, 1947, and ran until November 7, 1953, starring Richard Murdoch and Kenneth Horne with Sam Costa, Maurice Denham, Diana Morrison, and Barbara Leigh. The Dance Orchestra was conducted by Stanley Black. The show was written by Richard Murdoch and Kenneth Horne, and produced by Leslie Bridgmont.

EDUCATING ARCHIE ran from June 6, 1950, to February 17, 1960. A ventriloquist's dummy, Archie Andrews, was the star and his operator was Peter Brough. The opening shows starred Robert Moreton, Hattie Jacques, Julie Andrews, Petula Clark, The Tanner Sisters, The Hedley Ward Trio, and The Music Teachers. The show was written by Eric Sykes and Sid Colin, and produced by Roy Speer. Some episodes included Max Bygraves. The cast during the last shows included Sid James, Dick Emery and June Marlow. The script was then by Ronald Wolfe, Ronald Chesney and Marty Feldman. The show was produced by Geoffrey Owen.

THE GOON SHOW. On May 28, 1951, came the first of a new type of zany off-beat humour and the show ran until January 28, 1960. The first one was called CRAZY PEOPLE and it starred Harry Secombe, Peter Sellers, Michael Bentine, Spike Milligan, Margaret Lindsay and the Ray Ellington Quartet. To quote the *Radio Times* 'Material compiled by Spike Milligan'. Stanley Black conducted the Dance Orchestra and the show was produced by Dennis Main Wilson. Towards the end the cast changed a little, it was made up

137

of Peter Sellers, Harry Secombe, and Spike Milligan who wrote the script. The producer was John Browell.

HANCOCK'S HALF HOUR started on November 2, 1954, and ran until December 29, 1959. The cast of the first one included Tony Hancock with Moira Lister, Bill Kerr, Sid James, Gerald Campion and Kenneth Williams. The script (according to *Radio Times*) was written and adapted from 'The Junior Goldfish Keeper's Weekly' by Ray Galton and Alan Simpson. Producer: Dennis Main Wilson.

BEYOND OUR KEN, which started on July 1, 1958, and finished on February 16, 1964, was billed in the *Radio Times* as 'KENNETH HORNE insists that nothing is BEYOND OUR KEN and to prove it KENNETH WILLIAMS, HUGH PADDICK, BETTY MARSDEN, RON MOODY, PATRICIA LANCASTER and STANLEY UNWIN support him in a sort of radio show with the Malcolm Mitchell Trio, the BBC Revue Orchestra (leader Antony Gilbert), Conductor Harry Rabinowitz. Script by Eric Merriman and Barry Took. Produced by Jacques Brown.' The last of the series in 1964, written still by Eric Merriman, was cast as follows: Kenneth Horne, Kenneth Williams, Hugh Paddick, Betty Marsden, Bill Pertwee, the Fraser Hayes Four. Malcolm Lockyer conducted the BBC Revue Orchestra and 'a sort-of-announcer was Douglas Smith.' John Simmonds produced.

THE CLITHEROE KID with Jimmy Clitheroe, written and produced by James Casey, started on May 5, 1958, and the last episode was on August 13, 1972. During the run the cast varied but included Renée Houston, Peter Sinclair, Leonard Williams, Judith Daugherty, Nan Marriott-Watson, Judith Chalmers, Patricia Burke, Diana Day, Peter Goodright, Rosalie Williams, Tony Melody and Karal Gardner.

THE NAVY LARK opened on March 29, 1959, and ran until January 18, 1976. It was written by Lawrie Wyman and the cast included Dennis Price, Leslie Phillips, Jon Pertwee with Richard Caldicot, Heather Chasen, Michael Bates, Ronnie Barker and Tenniel Evans. In later episodes they were joined by Stephen Murray.

THE MEN FROM THE MINISTRY started in October 30, 1962, starring Richard Murdoch and Wilfred Hyde-White with Roy Dotrice, Diana Olsen, Edwin Apps, and David Graham. It was written and produced by Edward Taylor. The cast changed now and then and towards the end included Deryck Guyler, Norma Ronald, Ronald Baddiley, John Graham and David Nettheim. It was written then by Johnnie Mortimer, Brian Cooke and Edward Taylor, who produced the entire series.

ROUND THE HORNE ran from March 3, 1965, to June 9, 1968. It starred the avuncular Kenneth Horne. The brilliant writing was by Barry Took and Marty Feldman. The first episode included Kenneth Williams, Hugh Paddick, Betty Marsden and Bill Pertwee, and was produced by John Simmonds.

I'M SORRY, I'LL READ THAT AGAIN was first billed in October 4, 1965, as 'A new kind of laughing', and it ran until December 23, 1973. The cast of the first one, which was written by John Cleese, Tony Hendra, Graeme Garden, Johnnie Mortimer, Brian Cooke and Hugh Woodhouse, included Tim Brooke-Taylor, Graeme Garden, David Hatch, Jo Kendall and Bill Oddie, and before long John Cleese joined them at the microphone.

The first **NEWS HUDDLINES** was heard on November 3, 1976, it starred and stars Roy Hudd. The cast was Janet Brown and Chris Emmett. It was written by Chris Miller, Peter Spence, David Renwick 'and others'. The show is still running and the writers of the 1983 series included James Hendrie, Richard Quick, Charlie Adams, Nick Revell, Ian Brown, Jeremy Browne, Geoffrey Atkinson, Trevor McCallum, Trevor Cooper, John Collee, Martin Booth, John Lea, Peter Hickey 'and others'.

JUST A MINUTE started in 1950 as ONE MINUTE, PLEASE and starred Roy Plomley in the chair with Valerie Hobson, Kenneth Horne, Gilbert Harding, Gerard Hoffnung, Nan Kenway, Yvonne Arnaud and a host of others. Later, the game's inventor Ian Messiter, changed the title to JUST A MINUTE and under that title it has run since December 22, 1967. The cast of that first re-mix was Nicholas Parsons in the chair, where he still is, with Beryl Reid, Derek Nimmo, Clement Freud and Wilma Ewart on the panel. Today the only permanent panellist is Kenneth Williams, who is joined from time to time by Clement Freud, Derek Nimmo, Peter Jones, Sheila Hancock, Aimi MacDonald, Gyles Brandreth, Tim Rice and others. The original producer was David Hatch and the present (1984) producer is Pete Atkin.

THE HITCH-HIKER'S GUIDE TO THE GALAXY started on March 3, 1978 and was an immediate success. The billing in the *Radio Times* said 'An epic adventure in time and space including some helpful advice on how to see the Universe for less than 30 Altairian dollars a day.' The first episode starred Peter Jones with Simon Jones, Geoffrey McGivern, Bill Wallis, Jo Kendall and David Gooderson. The show was written by Douglas Adams and the first episode was produced by Simon Brett. The others, which ran spasmodically, were produced by Geoffrey Perkins.

WEEK ENDING had its first broadcast on April 4, 1970. It is the most popular comedy show with no studio audience. During a run up to an election it is always taken off the air. The original *Radio Times* billing was 'Michael Barratt looks back on the week's news and sees the funny side. Featuring Sean Arnold, Malcolm Hayes, Geoffrey Collins, Nigel Lambert, Frederick Treves and Basil Boothroyd reading next week's news. Script by Peter Spence. Produced by David Hatch and Simon Brett.'

Now we read that it is 'An irreverently critical look back on the week's news.' The cast is smaller: it includes Bill Wallace, David Tate, Sally Grace and Jon Glover. The writers include Ian Brown, James Hendrie, Max Alcock, Richard Quick, John Langdon, Paul B. Davies, Martin Booth, Alan Whiting and Peter Hickey.

Rules for life

1. If you don't go, you can't be late.
2. If the shoe fits, it's unfashionable.
3. No matter how lost you are, there you are.
4. The day you want to sell your soul, the price will drop because everyone's selling.
5. If you keep your mouth shut, you can't put your foot in it.
6. If you're uncertain, mumble.
7. If it moves, it's biology. If it smells, it's chemistry. If it won't work, it's physics.
8. Pessimistic anticipation will get bad results. Optimistic anticipation will get bad results.
9. The first 95% of the show can be written in 95% of the time. The last 5% will take another 95% of the time.
10. The greater the household income, the lower the proportion spent on food.
11. If you want a woman to listen, whisper.
12. Supply creates its own demand. (Say's law)
13. Whatever the political or tax system of a country, the distribution of income is much the same. (Pareto's law)
14. As population expands fast in times of plenty it eventually exceeds resources, so that ultimate hardship is inevitable. (Malthus' theory)
15. As soon as you are in the bath, the telephone will ring.
16. Whatever can be done wrong, will be. (At the worst possible time).
17. Bad money will drive good money out of circulation. (Gresham's law)
18. Every employee tends to rise to his level of incompetence. (The Peter Principle)
19. If facts conflict with theory, change the facts or the theory. (Spinoza's law)
20. When something fails to work and you demonstrate it to the repair man, it works better than ever.
21. Work expands to fill the time available for its completion. (Parkinson's law)

Stars thought to wear wigs

I had three hours to kill at Gatwick one day, so offered this list of stars in alphabetical order to those who were also waiting. I asked them to tick one name only.

STAR THOUGHT TO WEAR WIG	PERCENTAGE WHO THOUGHT HE DID
ERNIE WISE	40
BRUCE FORSYTH	21
BENNY HILL	12
BOB MONKHOUSE	10
PAUL DANIELS	7
SEAN CONNERY	6
LARRY GRAYSON	3
NICHOLAS PARSONS	1
JOHN CLEESE	0
EAMONN ANDREWS	0
KENNETH WILLIAMS	0
TREVOR MACDONALD	0
RONNIE BARKER	0
RONNIE CORBETT	0

Fishy facts

1. The teeth of a **white shark** are as hard as steel.
2. More people are killed each year by lightning than by **sharks**.
3. **Salmon** in Scotland have been seen to leap falls 5 metres (15 feet) high.
4. The bones of the **garfish** are green.
5. As the **white shark** is never ill and never has cancer, its antibodies are the subject of serious medical study.
6. The **shark's** sense of pain and incapacity must never be compared to that of man. The proof? A shark with a slit belly will turn and devour its own entrails.
7. The teeth of the **minnow** are not only in its mouth but in its throat too.
8. The eggs of the female **sea catfish** hatch in her mouth.

9. The **lung fish** out of water gets sleepier until it appears all but dead. It can survive in this state for three years. Put back into water it will revive and swim away.
10. The **salmon** finds its way back to fresh waters to spawn, first by the sun, then by the smell or taste of the water.
11. The **glutinous hagfish** has a strange way of getting a good mouthful of food. First it bites its prey, a dead or dying fish, with horny teeth on the sides of its tongue. Then, tying a knot in its own tail, it slides the knot down towards its mouth using it as a lever to wrench out the food it needs.
12. **Flying fish** do not fly for fun. They do it to avoid being eaten by bigger fish.

13. The **headlamp fish**, a cousin of the salmon, swims at great depths in the sea and has telescopic eyes, which work in a similar way to binoculars.
14. The female **herring** will lay some 150,000 eggs on the sea bed. There are no figures to show how many of the original 150,000 survive to become adult fish but a figure of 10 only has been suggested.

Things done for five minutes

1. A skylark can sustain a trill.
2. The sun was totally eclipsed from Indonesia on June 11th 1983 for 5 minutes.
3. A hippo walking submerged on the river bottom must surface after 5 minutes.
4. The human brain, starved of oxygen, will die after 5 minutes.
5. A swordfish can swim 9.5 km (6 miles) in 5 minutes.
6. It takes a lorry 5 minutes to spread rock salt on 1 kilometre (¾ mile) of average width frozen road.
7. A man standing on the Equator will travel 139.7 km (86.8 miles) east through the rotation of the earth in 5 minutes.
8. It takes 5 minutes to bleach clean a badly-stained coffee cup.

Famous mysteries

1. **THE MARY CELESTE**
   1872.
   The ship was found abandoned with no trace of the crew or what disaster befell them.
2. **THE DEVIL'S FOOTPRINTS**
   Devon, 1855.
   Extra large hoofprints were discovered in the snow. They covered over 100 miles (160 kilometres) going over roofs and apparently through walls. No explanation found.
3. **THE FLYING SCHOOLGIRL**
   Tunbridge Wells, 1876.
   A schoolgirl rose 50 feet (15 metres) in the air, spinning all the while, with no apparent cause. She died from her fall.
4. **PEOPLE WHO CAUGHT ALIGHT**
   (a) Pennsylvania, 1966.
   Dr John Bentley died from spontaneous self-combustion. All that remained were a pile of ashes and his left leg.
   (b) A 19 year old secretary at a disco with her boyfriend in London suddenly burst into flames, the fire coming through her back from inside her body. Coroner's verdict — 'Death by misadventure caused by fire of unknown origin.'
   (c) A cab driver was reported in the *Daily Telegraph* to have been totally consumed by fire in his cab.

5. THE FIRST BATTERY

Near Bagdad, 1936.
Workers found an earthenware jar containing a copper cylinder which enclosed an iron rod. The top had been sealed with bitumen and on close examination the rod had been eaten away by acid. Identified as a primitive electric battery, dating from about 250 BC.

6. BALL LIGHTNING

1975.
Reports described a blue, fuzzy-edged ball of light which came into the house via a window, burnt those who touched it, then disappeared or exploded.

7. SPRING-HEELED JACK

January, February and March 1837.
A weird apparition in the shape of a tall man with glowing red eyes and who breathed blue fire. He was seen to appear, jump over houses and vanish on various occasions. Those who saw him or were touched by him were sometimes badly hurt.

English place names and their Roman counterparts

For about 3½ centuries Britain was a province of the Roman Empire. The first Roman troops landed in 55 BC and during the succeeding centuries they built roads, bridges and towns. They introduced cleanliness. They took baths and showed us the advantages of them. They introduced law and order. It was decided that no further troops should be sent here in 410 AD., after the governing of Britain had become increasingly troublesome. From 4-500 AD we forgot our manners, we no longer built houses or bathrooms, and indeed even in the early 20th century houses were still being built without bathrooms. The well-founded Roman roads mostly became overgrown and we even forgot the names given to the towns. But they were not completely forgotten: here they are.

ENGLISH NAME	ROMAN NAME
ALDBURGH	Isurium
BATH	Aquae Sulis
BROUGH	Peturaria
CAERLEON	Isca Silurum
CAERWENT	Vents Silurum
CANTERBURY	Durovernum
CARLISLE	Luguvalium
CHELMSFORD	Caesaromagus
CHESTER	Deva
CHICHESTER	Noviomagus
CIRENCESTER	Corinium
COLCHESTER	Camulodunum
DONCASTER	Danum
DORCHESTER	Durnovaria
DOVER	Dubris
EXETER	Isca Dumnoniorum
GLOUCESTER	Glevum
LANCASTER	Lunecastrum
LEICESTER	Ratae Coritanorum
LINCOLN	Lindum
LONDON	Londinium
MANCHESTER	Mancunium
NEWCASTLE	Pons Aelius

ENGLISH NAME	ROMAN NAME
NEWSTEAD	Trimontium
PEVENSEY	Anderida
ROCHESTER	Durobrivae
ST. ALBANS	Verulamium
SALISBURY	Sorbiodunum
SILCHESTER	Cavella Atrebatum
WINCHESTER	Venta Belgarum
WORCESTER	Wigornia
WROXETER	Viroconium
YARMOUTH	Magna Gernemutha
YORK	Eboracum

Vogue words

These, like clichés, are over-used words. They are often written or spoken without much thought and do not, I think, improve the language.

1. Privatization.
2. Burglarized.
3. Basically.
4. Supportive.
5. Live-in girl/boy friend
6. Victoriana.
7. Hospitalization.
8. Preppy. (Upper class adolescent.)
9. Memorabilia.
10. Breakthrough. (Meaning 'discovery' or 'achievement'.)
11. Blueprint. (Meaning 'plan'.)
12. Viable. (Meaning 'workable'.)
13. Redundant. (Meaning 'superfluous'.)
14. Integrate. (Meaning 'combine'.)
15. Ceiling. (Meaning 'limit'.)

Animals originally foreign to our shores but now naturalized

Using the word 'naturalized' here is a reference to animals which have been imported one way or another and which have settled down to live in the wild state. This list deals only with vertebrates.

1. **The Canada goose;** possibly introduced by or before Charles II for St James's Park London, is common throughout our islands.

2. **The grey squirrel;** this pretty creature from North America was almost certainly first released in some woods near Macclesfield in 1876.

3. **The edible dormouse;** was imported by the Romans.

4. **Bennett's wallabies;** these presented a problem at the outbreak of war in 1939, because it was difficult to confine and feed them, so collector Captain Henry Brocklehurst set them free. They can now be seen in Derbyshire, Sussex and Staffordshire.

5. **Escaped hamsters** are capable of survival in the wild. They have been reported wandering, well fed and happy in Finchley, Barrow-in-Furness, Bootle and other widely separated places.

6. **The brownish yellow coypu;** originally from South America, they were brought to our islands in 1929 for their fur, but it was not long before they escaped and naturalized themselves.

7. **Two Himalayan porcupines** made their way unobserved from Pine Valley Wildlife Park in Devon in 1969. They are now established in several parts of Britain.

8. **Rabbits** are not native to the British Isles. They originally came from central Europe, yet before the 1953 myxomatosis outbreak, they could be seen in all rural and semi-rural areas.

9. **The Little Owl** is the smallest owl in the British isles being only about 22 cm (9 inches) from beak to tail. The first to arrive were bought in Rome by the owner of Walton Hall, Squire Charles Waterton, in Yorkshire in May 1842.

10. **The Edible Frog,** like the dormouse and rabbit, may well have been introduced to these islands by the Romans but there is no record to support this theory. The first recorded introduction of this creature, whose hind legs taste rather like chicken, was in 1837. They were brought here by George Berney of Norfolk, who had the then considerable task of transporting two hundred of them and a great deal of spawn from Paris. It seems he had a fixation about the creatures, because in 1841 he brought over an undisclosed number from Brussels and in 1842 he managed to transport over 1,300 which he put into the fens at Foulden. It is not known even vaguely how many of their descendants have croaked. It is known that they may have a tough time living in this unpredictable climate and would almost certainly have died out if it were not for others like George Berney, who enjoy bringing them here.

Nicholas Parson's list of eleven exciting batsmen

What is it that makes the game of cricket so unique? To my mind it is connected with the art of batmanship. Whenever you hear people talking about the game, and great moments or occasions that they have witnessed, it is invariably concerned with batsmen ... great innings that they have witnessed ... record scores ... fine partnerships ... incredible strokes ... exceptional batting technique ... and so on. I think this is because it requires a special character to be a successful batsman. It is the only activity in any sport where if you make a mistake you rarely have a second chance. For this reason when a great batsman walks to the wicket there is an air of excitement and expectancy that you will not experience in any other game, and when that batsman is in form and striking the ball well his personality and presence so dominates and lifts the game, it becomes almost a theatrical event and something that you remember and talk about later.

It is those batsmen, with this unique quality of personality and presence, that I have included in my list of eleven. The eleven I have chosen I have had the pleasure of watching at sometime or other, during a lifetime of following cricket since a schoolboy. In no order of merit, consistency or records broken, they are:

Don Bradman	Australia
Patsy Hendren	Middlesex and England
Frank Woolley	Kent and England
Walter Hammond	Gloucestershire and England
Harold Gimblett	Somerset and England
Everton Weekes	West Indies
Denis Compton	Middlesex and England
Keith Millar	Australia
Garfield Sobers	West Indies
Barry Richards	Hampshire and South Africa
Ian Botham	Somerset and England

My list of curious musical instruments

By Christine Messiter, Principal Flute to the BBC Symphony Orchestra.

1. **Hurdy-Gurdy.** The real hurdy-gurdy was a stringed instrument, the size of a large violin, with many strings, some of which only vibrated in sympathy with the others and were called 'drones'. The others were played by one hand depressing keys to stop them along their length and the other hand turning a crank which revolved a wooden wheel which touched the strings much like a violin bow.

2. **Cimbalom.** Looking like a trapezoid, sturdy, post-war dining table, the cimbalom is best known for the tremolo chords and melodies associated with Hungarian gypsy bands. The strings stretched out horizontally inside are struck with wooden hammers, covered with leather or wool.

3. **Racket.** About ten vertical channels were bored into this wooden sausage-shaped instrument. These were alternately connected top and bottom to form an extremely long tube. Holes were then bored from the outside to meet the tube for the fingers to cover. A double reed sat on the top.

4. **Serpents.** This wiggly-shaped instrument was made of wood, bound with leather and had a mouthpiece like that of a trombone that was attached to a metal crook.

5. **Glass Harmonica.** This strange instrument is constructed of bowls made of glass and played by stroking the rims with wet fingers (you may have tried this with a wine glass). Today the bowls are not filled with water to change their pitch, this is achieved by their different size.

6. **Contrabass Sarrusophone.** It was designed by one Monsieur Sarrus, a French army bandmaster, in 1856, who wished it to replace the oboes and bassoons in his bands. Made out of metal, with double reeds, they were not delicate instruments, but powerful and incisive in sound.

7. **Jews Harp.** An open-ended, rounded piece of wood or metal, which has a vibrating metal tongue, is inserted into the mouth. By twanging the metal tongue with the finger or jerking it with a piece of string and simultaneously changing the shape of one's mouth, the player can make a variety of notes.

8. **Theremin.** This electrical instrument, invented by Professor Leon Theremin in the 1920s, changes pitch when a metal ring is passed from one end of a metal rod to the other, both of which are connected to electrical circuits. The player's other hand moves above the metal rod and controls the volume. It has an eerie siren sound.

9. **Bassett horn.** This rather self-effacing member of the clarinet family is not a horn at all, but a large clarinet with a metal bell.

10. **Wind machine.** A terribly exciting instrument to listen to, that sends cold shivers down one's spine. A large cylindrical framework, covered with silk is turned by handle within an outer wooden cylinder. The friction between the two causes incredibly authentic gales and even gentle breezes to waft over the orchestra.

A list of threes

1. 3 Little Maids. Yum-Yum, Peep-Bo and Pitti-Sing (Gilbert and Sullivan)
2. 3 men in a tub. Butcher, baker and candlestick maker.
3. 3 Musketeers. Athos, Porthos and Aramis. (Joined later, according to Dumas, by D'Artagnan)
4. 3 Wise Monkeys. Mizaru, See no Evil, Kikazuru, Hear no Evil, Iwazaru, Speak no Evil.
5. 3 Wise Men. Caspar, Melchior, Balthazar.
6. 3 Rs. Reading, 'riting and 'rithmetic.
7. 3 Cardinal virtues. Faith, Hope and Charity.
8. 3 parts of man. Mind, body and spirit.
9. 3. Pythagoras's perfect number, symbolising the beginning, the middle and the end. When Jean-Luc Goddard, the French film producer, was asked whether he felt films should have a beginning, a middle and an end, he replied 'yes — but not necessarily in that order'.
10. 3 legged mare. The old gallows at Tyburn (Marble Arch, London) was made up of three wooden supports meeting at the top from where the rope hung.

Items handed in to Heathrow lost property office

It's amazing what people have, let alone what they lose.

1. A dog's head pickled in alcohol.
2. A Spanish Astra revolver.
3. 3 pairs of knickers.
4. 47 umbrellas.
5. A piranha fish in glass bowl.
6. A wedding cake.
7. 2 perambulators.
8. A book called 'How to Improve your Memory'.
9. A wheel chair.
10. A crematorium urn, empty. This is reminiscent of a Tokyo railway lost property office receiving a crematorium urn with someone's ashes still in it.

A list of wrong names

1. **TURKEY.** The bird comes from North America not Turkey. (In Turkey it is known as 'The American bird.')

2. **BLINDWORM.** This is not a worm nor is it blind. It is a legless lizard.
3. **THE FOUR ELEMENTS,** earth, fire, air and water. These are not elements.
4. **SALTS OF LEMON.** This has nothing to do with a lemon. It is potassium quadroxalate.
5. **A TIN CAN.** This would be very expensive if it were really tin, which is a rare and costly metal. 'Tin cans' are usually made of bright mild steel with some anti-rust coating.
6. **GALVANIZED METAL** is not 'galvanized'. It is dipped into and so coated with molten zinc, without the use of electricity.
7. **SILVER PAPER** is not silver but some other metal. There are so many varieties today it would be difficult to give a comprehensive list.
8. **VENTRILOQUISM.** This word comes from the Latin 'Venter — Stomach' and 'Loqui — Speak' which compounded should mean that a ventriloquist speaks from his stomach. However, he does not.

9. **JERUSALEM ARTICHOKE** has nothing to do with Jerusalem. The name is a corruption of the Italian word 'girasole'. Girasole is another word for sunflower and the vegetable looks very like this when growing.
10. **CLEOPATRA'S NEEDLE.** There is one in London on the Embankment and one in New York. Neither of these stone obelisks has anything to do with Cleopatra. Note the dates which prove it. Cleopatra 69 – 30 BC. Both obelisks were erected by Thotmes III in about 1500 BC.

Somnolent themes

1. In the northern hemisphere we sleep more soundly during March than at any other time of the year.
2. We sleep better when it is raining than when it is fine (assuming that you sleep indoors and not in a field).
3. Children grow more when lying down than when standing up.
4. From the moment the light is out at bedtime, the average person takes seven minutes to fall asleep.
5. A person who smokes does not dream as much as a non-smoker.
6. You do not enjoy two out of every five dreams. The other three certainly make up for it.
7. Did your foot go to sleep when the rest of you stayed awake? If it did, that curious phenomenon is called *taresthesia*.
8. Your bed should be 20 cm (8 inches) longer than you.
9. Pyjamas originated in India and were not intended as night attire but as costumes in which to keep cool when not working.
10. One pillow is conducive to sound sleep, once you get used to it. People who use two or more pillows do not sleep well. They also suffer more headaches.
11. If you have a problem getting to sleep, alcohol will seem to solve it, but you will wake up sooner.
12. Insomniacs who try going for a twenty minute walk before going to bed will mostly stop being insomniacs.
13. Single women dream more than married women.
14. Men do not dream as long or as often as women.

Curious health facts

1. If you inherit money, win the pools or become the chairman of a great company, etc., you may expect to get ill.
2. Similarly if you suffer a loss of a great friend, spouse, finance or job, you can expect to get ill.
3. Only twenty per cent of serious road accidents happen in poor visibility. The majority happen when visibility is excellent.
4. If you have been badly treated, snubbed or belittled as a child, you have a greater chance of worldly success, than if you have had a kind upbringing.
5. Between 40% and 60% of medicine prescribed by doctors is thrown away.
6. People who sit on the ground instead of on chairs do not get varicose veins.
7. If you live to 75, you will almost certainly catch 150 colds before you are through with life.
8. Sound dulls your sense of smell and taste. 'Noses' who work in scent factories have to give their sniff of approval or otherwise in soundproofed rooms. If you want to appreciate a good wine, turn the radio, television and in-laws off and savour it quietly.

9. Vaseline was invented by Robert Chesebrough when he was 22. He lived to 96 and said his long life was because he ate a spoonful of Vaseline every day.
10. To cure a common cold, according to Dr Yinder Urban in the Prague Medical Tribune, simply put both of your forearms simultaneously into a basin of water for an hour keeping the water at a constant temperature of 104°F or 40°C. Next day you will not have your cold. I do not believe it but it is worth a try, if you can manage it.
11. 73% of the population has at some time suffered from backache.

Unmusical items which have been used as musical instruments

Some of these things will be recognised by readers as having been used in Hoffnung Music Festivals.

1. Vacuum cleaners.
2. Blowing across the tops of old-fashioned stone bedroom hot water bottles.
3. Shot guns.
4. Spoons.
5. Washboards rubbed with thimbles.
6. Lengths of hosepipe played as trumpets.
7. Garden watering cans also played as trumpets.
8. Sandpaper rubbed with sandpaper.
9. Cork fired from a pop-gun.
10. Inflated balloons pulled by the neck to produce a squeak.
11. Soda water being expelled from a syphon into a glass.
12. A comb wrapped in tissue paper, then blown like a mouth organ to produce a humming sound.
13. In the Joseph Strauss Champagne Polka, a bottle of champagne is carefully timed to be opened at a precise beat with a good loud pop.
14. The lion's roar is in rare pieces of music and is frequently reproduced by pulling a rough rope through a hole in a drum.

Items stolen by office workers

This list comes from two large companies which, because they want to preserve good staff relations, have sworn me to secrecy on penalty of death. The curious point of the list is that it was originally two lists, one from each company, but they are coincidentally identical.

1. Pens, both felt tip and ball point.
2. Stationery, including folders and clip files.
3. Sticky tape.
4. Telephone calls.
5. Paper grips.
6. Time. (Arriving late. Staying out too long for lunch. Going to the cloakroom well before time in order to be ready to dash out at leaving time.)

A crazy alphabet list

This alphabet was popular with music hall comics in the late 1930s. It has been updated as some of the original material would have no meaning today. Say it out loud and you should get a word, phrase or even a person's name.

A	FOR 'ORSES
B	FOR MUTTON
C	FOR THIGHLANDERS
D	FOR ENTIAL
E	FOR ADAM
F	FOR VESCENT
G	FOR POLICE
H	FOR EXPERIENCE
I	FOR NOVELLO
J	FOR ORANGES
K	FOR RESTAURANT
L	FOR LEATHER
M	FOR SIS
N	FOR LOPE
O	FOR MY SHOULDER
P	FOR A WHISTLE
Q	FOR A BUS
R	FOR MARIA
S	FOR RANTZEN
T	FOR TWO
U	FOR MIZZAM
W	FOR QUITS
X	FOR BREAKFAST
Y	FOR HUSBAND
Z	FOR BREEZES

Things done in five minutes

1. Water can be made drinkable after boiling it for 5 minutes.
2. If the oven is at 350 degrees Fahrenheit a cake will start to rise after 5 minutes.
3. After 5 minutes in a photographic darkroom normal eyes will be accustomed to the red light.

4. A baked Alaska will be cooked after 5 minutes in the oven.
5. An automatic pile driver takes 5 minutes to drive a pile 3 metres (10 feet) into clay.
6. A skilled hypnotist takes 5 minutes to put a patient into a trance.
7. After working for 5 minutes a glass marble factory will have produced 1,000 marbles.
8. A motorist can change a front wheel of a car.
9. A practised knitter can make 500 hand stitches.
10. Your heart will pump 270 litres (60 gallons) of blood if you are exercising.
11. An educated reader can take in 1,500 printed words.
12. An orchestra conductor will use up 20 calories.
13. This is the time taken to milk a cow.
14. A woman fencer will win her match if she makes 4 touches in 5 minutes.
15. Your heart beats 375 times in 5 minutes.
16. A stage dancer will lose 12 calories dancing for 5 minutes.
17. After washing and shaving the average man can dress himself in 5 minutes, provided he doesn't lose his socks.

Common expressions and how we came by them

1. **A LAUGHING STOCK.** A village nuisance in the old days would be put in the stocks and have old eggs and rubbish thrown at him while others looked on and laughed.
2. **A RULE OF THUMB.** A generalization as a result of taking a casual measurement with the thumb.
3. **DOUBLE DEALING.** Dealing alternately from the top of the pack and deceitfully from the bottom of the pack.
4. **HE BEAT ME HOLLOW.** This is a corruption of 'He beat me wholly'.
5. **THEY BEAT THE DAYLIGHTS OUT OF HIM.** His daylights being his eyes.
6. **THE HAIR OF THE DOG.** A false idea that another glass of the drink that poisoned you last night will cure your hangover today. This is from an old superstition that a dog bite can be cured by putting a hair of the same dog in or on the wound.

7. **THAT STORY SHOULD BE TAKEN WITH A GRAIN OF SALT.** In other words the story is not to be trusted but might be swallowed if helped down by a little salt, after the idea that some foods are more palatable with added salt.
8. **WE EGGED HIM ON.** Nothing to do with eggs; it is a corruption of the word 'edge' and should be 'We edged him on'.
9. **IT'S NOT WORTH THE CANDLE.** In other words, it's not worth the expense of lighting a candle to see it.
10. **BACK TO SQUARE ONE.** From radio commentaries on football when the listener was supplied with a squared map of the field. The position of the ball and the players could be identified.
11. **HOLD YOUR HORSES.** In other words, wait for further orders. The phrase originated with the Royal Horse Artillery.
12. **PULL THE OTHER ONE, IT HAS BELLS ON.** From old court jesters who wore bells on both legs.
13. **WE ARE NOT AMUSED.** Said to someone who has made a silly or rude joke. It was supposedly said first by Queen Victoria, but there is no record of her having said it.
14. **MONEY TALKS.** According to Eric Partridge originally this was from Torriano's 'Man prates, but gold speaks', 1666.

A list of all rights

1. The Statue of Liberty carries her torch in her right hand.
2. Rodin's sculpture 'The Thinker' rests his head on his right hand.
3. Two ships approaching each other must pass right side to right side. (Starboard to starboard.)
4. The right side of your brain controls the left side of your body.
5. In ancient Rome a boy was made to stand near the door of a rich house to warn those coming in that they must enter with the right foot as this was more auspicious. They had to put the right foot forward.
6. A trivet has three legs so it will not wobble. Hence the expression 'right as a trivet'.
7. The word 'dextrous' has its roots in the Latin for right (while 'sinister' comes from the Latin for left). This, in olden times, meant that right handed people were 'all right'. Left handed people could be considered 'sinister'. This gave rise to the cruel old fashioned habit of making left handed children

write with the right hand.

8. The right feet and hands of most people are slightly larger than the left.

9. The following flat fish have both eyes on the right side: halibut; long rough dab; dab; plaice; flounder; witch; lemon sole; sole and solenette.

10. The name 'right whale' referred originally to the Greenland or bowhead and the black right whale. Both were once considered to be the 'right' whales to hunt because of their value, slowness and buoyancy after death.

11. Long John Silver's good leg is his right leg.

12. Ray Allen's dummy, Lord Charles, wears his monocle in his right eye.

13. Peter Falk's right eye is glass.

14. German women wear their wedding rings on their right hands.

15. Doctor Strangelove's crippled hand which made the Nazi salute was his right hand.

16. Few men part their hair on the right.

17. A miner's right is an Australian term for a licence to prospect for gold.

18. A right hand man is a confidential and valued assistant. He was originally the man to the right of a line of cavalry who carried great responsibility.

Some first names with their origins – are you here?

Many varied spellings of the same name have been left out for the sake of brevity. Only the most usual or interesting names have been included. The feminine forms, when directly taken from the masculine and vice versa follow the definition. Our apologies if you have been left out.

A

1.	ADAM	With a red coloured skin
2.	ADRIAN	From the Adriatic. ADRIANA
3.	ALEXANDER	A defending man. ALEXANDRA
4.	ALFRED	Great peace. ALFREDA
5.	ALICE	Noble sort
6.	AMY	Loved
	sometimes AIMÉE	
7.	ANDREW	Manly. ANDREA
8.	ARNOLD	With the ability of an eagle
9.	ARTHUR	A bear

B

10.	BARBARA	Strange, alien
11.	BARRY	Spear carrier
12.	BASIL	Regal
13.	BENJAMIN	Son of my sorrow
14.	BRIDGET	The high one
15.	BRUCE	Brave

C

16.	CEDRIC	A name invented by Walter Scott
17.	CHARLES	A man. CAROL, CHARLOTTE
18.	CHRISTOPHER	Carrying Christ in the heart
19.	CLARA, CLARE	Bright and clear
20.	CYRIL	Lord and master

D

21.	DANIEL	Whom God has judged
22.	DAPHNE	Bay or laurel
23.	DAVID	Originally 'darling', later 'friend' DAVINA

24.	DEBORAH	A bee
25.	DEN(N)IS	Of Dionysos. DENISE
26.	DEREK	Ruler of the people
27.	DIANA	Latin version of the Greek name Artemis, the Moon goddess
28.	DOROTHY	Gift from God
29.	DOUGLAS	Dark blue

E

30.	EDGAR	Rich and carrying a spear
31.	EDMUND	Rich protector
32.	EDWARD	Rich guardian
33.	ELIZABETH	My God is satisfaction
34.	EMMA	Whole
35.	ERIC	Ruler. ERICA
36.	ERNEST	Earnest, vigorous. ERNESTINE
37.	EVE, EVA	Lively

F

38.	FELICITY	Happiness. FELIX
39.	FIONA	Invented by author of 'Fiona MacLeod', William Sharp
40.	FLEUR	Invented by author of 'Forsyte Saga', John Galsworthy
41.	FRANCIS	A Frenchman (The father of St Francis of Assisi was travelling in France at the time of the baby's birth.) FRANCES

G

42.	GEOFFREY	Peace
43.	GEORGE	Tiller of the soil, a farmer. GEORGINA, GEORGIANA
44.	GERALD	Ruling with a spear. GERALDINE
45.	GRACE	Grace. Similar to Faith, Hope and Charity which were the Victorian names given to children in the hope that such virtues might be imbued in them
46.	GWEN	White

H

47.	HAROLD	A leader of a strong army

48.	HELEN (A)	The bright one
49.	HENRY	Ruler of the house. HENRIETTA, HARRIET
50.	HILARY	Cheerful
51.	HOWARD	Protector of the soul
52.	HUGH, HUGO	Heart

|

53.	IAN	John
54.	IRENE	Peace
55.	ISABEL(LA)	Elizabeth

J

56.	JAMES	He seized the heel, or supplanted. JAQUELINE
57.	JASPER	After one of the wise men, Jasper (Caspar) see page 153.
58.	JOHN	God has favoured. First born JOAN, JANE, JANET (diminutive of JANE), JEAN, JEANETTE, JENNY
59.	JONATHAN	God has given us a son
60.	JOSEPH	May God give us more children. JOSEPHINE
61.	JUDITH	A Jewess
62.	JUSTIN	From 'just and fair'. JUSTINA, JUSTINE

K

63.	KATHERINE	Torture, from St Katharine who was broken on the wheel prior to being beheaded. Similar names are derivative e.g. KATE, CATHERINE, KATHLEEN, KAY, KITTY
64.	KEITH	From the place names of several Scottish villages.
65.	KENNETH	Comely
66.	KEVIN	Comely birth

L

67.	LAURENCE, LAWRENCE	From laurus, a bay tree
68.	LESLIE	(Probably) gladness. LESLEY
69.	LEWIS, LOUIS	A fighter. LOUISE

70.	LINDA	Originally German from the linden tree

M

71.	MABEL	Lovable
72.	MALCOLM	Servant to Columb
73.	MARK	Derived from Mars, God of War
74.	MARGARET	A pearl. Curiously related to margarine 'a pearl like substance', which it is before added colour
75.	MARY	A wished-for child
76.	MATTHEW	Gift of God
77.	MAURICE	A Moor
78.	MAVIS	From the song thrush, the mavis
79.	MELANIE	Black
80.	MELODY	Tuneful
81.	MICHAEL	Who is like the Lord
82.	MILLICENT	Strong worker
83.	MIRABEL	Marvellous
84.	MIRANDA	Shakespearian invention (The Tempest) but also Latin for 'worthy to be admired'
85.	MIRIAM	Desirable
86.	MONA	Noble
87.	MURIEL	The bright sea

N

88.	NAOMI	Pleasure
89.	NICHOLAS	Victory for the people. NICOLA, NICOLETTE
90.	NIGEL	Champion
91.	NOEL	Born on Christmas day. NOELLE
92.	NORMAN	A man from the north. A northman. NORMA

O

93.	OLIVER	One who tends olive groves. OLIVIA, OLIVE

P

94.	PAMELA	Invented for 'Arcadia' by Philip Sydney
95.	PATRICK	A patriarch. Head of the family. A nobleman. PATRICIA, PATSY

96.	PAUL	From the Latin 'paulus' small. PAULA, PAULINA, PAULINE
97.	PETER	A stone. PETRONELLA
98.	PHILIP	One who loves horses. PHILLIPPA
99.	PHYLLIS	A sad name as it comes from the Greek for 'leafy' who was a girl who hanged herself for love and became a tree

Q

100.	QUENTIN	Fifth born

R

101.	RACHEL	A ewe lamb
102.	RALPH	Taking counsel from a wolf
103.	RENE	Born again. RENÉE
104.	RICHARD	A tough ruler
105.	ROBERT	Bright fame. ROBERTA
106.	ROGER	One who gained fame with his spear
107.	RONALD	Strong
108.	ROSALIND	Old German (r)hos 'horse' and the linden tree
109.	ROSEMARY	Various meanings: 1. The sweet smelling herb. 2. A combination of rose, the flower, and Mary. 3. Old German (r)hos 'horse', and so a horse-woman called Mary. See Mary.
110.	ROY	Two possibilities. 1. From the French 'roi' a king. 2. It is a Gaelic name meaning 'red'.

S

111.	SAMUEL	A name of God
112.	SARAH	Princess
113.	SEBASTIAN	A man from the city of Sebastia
114.	SHIRLEY	From the place, Shirley. It is both a male and a female name.
115.	SOPHIA	Wise
116.	STELLA	A star
117.	STEPHEN	A crown. STEPHANIE
118.	SUSAN	A lily
119.	SYLVIA	From the Latin 'woody'. SILVESTER

120.	TERESA	Possibly 'a reaper' (Doubtful)
121.	THELMA	Invented by Marie Corelli for her novel of the same name.
122.	THOMAS	A twin. TOMASINE, TOMASINA
123.	TIMOTHY	Honour and respect
124.	TOBIAS, TOBY	God is good

U

125.	URSULA	A she-bear

V

126.	VERA	One with faith
127.	VERONICA	The true image. A reference to the shroud which is said to have taken on the true likeness of Jesus.
128.	VICTOR	A conqueror. VICTORIA. VICKY
129.	VINCENT	A conqueror
130.	VIVIAN	Alive. VIVIENNE

W

131.	WALTER	A ruler of the people
132.	WENDY	Invented by J. M. Barrie for the play 'Peter Pan'
133.	WILLIAM	A shining helmet. WILMOT, WILHELMINA

Z

134.	ZOE	Eve

A remarkable list from the Guinness Book of Records

This list, by its nature, is subjective. There are so many different remarkable facts to be browsed through, even without the instances of the tallest man or the fattest woman, that another writer would certainly make another list. By that token, 20 writers would make 20 lists and it would be unlikely that two items would coincide.

1. 'Wheelie. Capt Michael J. Brundage drove his Honda XL-250 on the Interstate 20 Highway west of Forth Worth, Texas on its back wheel for a 52.1 km (32.4 mile) "wheelie" on 23 July, 1982.'
2. 'The most brainless (for its size) creature was the "Stegosaurus" ("plated reptile"), which measured up to 9 metres (30 feet) in total length and weighed 1¾ tonnes, had a walnut-sized brain weighing only 70 g (2½ oz), which represented 0,004 of one per cent of its body weight (compare with 1.88 per cent for a human).'
3. 'The oldest known map of any kind is a clay tablet depicting the River Euphrates flowing through northern Mesopotamia, Iraq, dated c. 3800 B.C.'
4. 'The youngest recorded commercially published author is Dorothy Straight (b. 25 May, 1958) of Washington D.C. who wrote *How the World Began* in 1962 aged 4 which was published in August 1964 by Pantheon Books, New York.'
5. 'The maritime sovereign country with the shortest coastline is Monaco with 5.61 km (3.49 miles) excluding piers and breakwaters.'
6. 'The world's narrowest street is in Port Isaac, Cornwall at the junction of Temple Bar and Dolphin Street. It is popularly known as "Squeeze-belly alley" and is 49 cm (19⁵⁄₁₆ in) wide at its narrowest point.'
7. 'Message in a bottle. The longest recorded interval between drop and pick up is 64 years between 7 August, 1910 ("please write to Miss Gladys Potter") in Grand Lade and August, 1974 from Lake Huron. Miss Potter was traced as Mrs Oliver Scheid, 76 of Columbus, Ohio.'
8. 'The last use of corporal punishment in one of H.M. Prisons was on June 26, 1962 and it was abolished in the United Kingdom by the Criminal Justice Act, 1967. The treadmill

which 14 prisons operated in 1878 was finally suspended on 1 April, 1902. Men on the 36 man wheel at Northallerton, Yorkshire raised themselves 2,937 metres (9,639 feet) in an 8 hour day.'

9. 'The world's first shopping centre was Roland Park Shopping Center, Baltimore, Maryland built in 1896.'

10. 'Entertainment. Shortest run *World*. The shortest run on record was that of *The Intimate Revue* at the Duchess Theatre, London, on 11 March, 1930. Anything which could go wrong did. With scene changes taking up to 20 minutes apiece, the management scrapped seven scenes to get the finale on before midnight. The run was described as "half a performance".'

11. 'The oldest nudist resort is Der Freilichtpark, Klingberg, West Germany established in 1903.'

12. 'The commonest pub name in Britain is "Red Lion" of which there are probably just more than 1,000.'

13. 'The hotel with the most rooms in the world is the 12 storey Hotel Rossiya in Moscow, USSR, with 3,200 rooms providing accommodation for 5,350 guests opened in 1967. It would thus require more than 8½ years to spend one night in each room. In addition there is a 21 storey "Presidential" tower in the central courtyard. The hotel employs about 3,000 people, and has 93 lifts. The ballroom is reputed to be the world's largest. Muscovites are not permitted as residents while foreigners are charged 16 times more than the low rate charged to USSR officials.'

14. 'The highest number of "takes" for a TV commercial is 28 by Pat Coombs, the comedienne . . . Her explanation was "Every time we came to the punch line I just could not remember the name of the product".'

15. 'Most hanging attempts. In 1803 it was reported that Joseph Samuels was reprieved in Sydney, Australia after three unsuccessful attempts to hang him in which the rope twice broke.'

16. 'The oldest army in the world is the 83-strong Swiss Guard in the Vatican City, with a regular foundation dating back to 21 January, 1506. Its origins, however, extend back before 1400.'

17. 'The most productive goldmine in Britain was Clogan St. David's, Powys, Wales, in which county gold was discovered in 1836. This mine yielded 120,000 fine oz. in 1854-1914.'

18. 'Underwater Violinist. The only violinist to surmount the problems of playing the violin underwater has been Mark Gottlieb. Submerged in Evergreen State College swimming bath in Olympia, Washington, U.S.A. in March 1975, he gave a submarine rendition of Handel's Water Music. He is still working on the problem of bow speed and *détaché*.'

19. 'The shortest correspondence on record was that between Victor Marie Hugo (1802-85) and his publisher Hurst and Blackett in 1862. The author was on holiday and anxious to know how his new novel *Les Misérables* was selling. He wrote "?". The reply was "!".'

Classic magic tricks

1. **Phantasmagoria.** The magician conjured up a transparent ghost on stage and then would walk through it and slice it with his sword.

2. **Cups and balls.** Three pebbles are placed, one at a time under three cups. The magic part is that the pebbles then appear all together under one cup or even turn up in the magician's mouth.

3. **Learned geese or reading dogs.** A whole variety of creatures have been trained to respond to movements by the trainer which could not be perceived by the audience. Outwardly they appear to be making intelligent decisions (see Sieur Rea, page 173).

4. **The automaton chess player,** which would play and beat any member of the audience. The chess boards were always mounted on a large cube which concealed a good, but small chess player.

5. **Rabbits from top hats.** This trick was first performed in 1830. Regrettably history does not record the name of the conjuror.

6. **Sawing a lady in half.** First performed by P. T. Selbit (see page 174). A magazine of the day said that if anyone stole the invention from the conjuror, the thief would be put in a box, cut in half and not restored.

7. **Levitation,** in which a person is raised off the ground without apparent support. A hoop is usually passed over the floating figure to 'prove' absence of support.

8. **Black Art.** The stage is surrounded by illumination. The backdrop is black material. Assistants can walk about dressed in black without being seen. Any white object is immediately visible. This means that, if, for example, a large white egg in a white egg cup is covered in black velvet, this can be snatched off by an assistant, with the result that the egg appears as if by magic.

Magicians and conjurors

1. In 1810 **Sieur Rea** (from London) astonished many at the Town Hall, Weymouth with his 'Little Scientific Spanish Pony', which would tap with a hoof the suit and number of a chosen card and do similar tricks.

2. There have been many magicians called Bosco but the original was **Bartolomeo Bosco** who, according to the early 19th century papers of the day, 'could conjure away a house as easily as a nutmeg'. He was Italy's master of the cups and balls (see page 172), and these were carved on his tombstone, when he died in Dresden in 1863.

3. In 1822 the Englishman **Ingleby**, who claimed to be the 'Emperor of all the Conjurors', advertised that he could change the colour of a bowl of sand by breathing on it. The colours were called for by the audience.

4. In 1842 Britain saw the Austrian **Herr Louis Dobler**, who opened his act by firing a pistol. Immediately some 200 candles on the stage would become lighted. He performed at Windsor Castle for Queen Victoria and when he died in Austria in 1864 Doblergasse in Vienna was named after him: the only street in the world to bear the name of a conjuror.

5. The father of modern magic was **Robert Houdin** who until he was 40 had been an expert watchmaker and mechanic. He opened his 'Soirées Fantastiques' in Paris in 1845. His background as watchmaker and mechanic was ideal for an inventor of magical apparatus. He was the inventor of the much seen illusion where a person lies horizontally in space with just an elbow resting on an upright pole. His illusions are still copied. In 1856 the French Government asked him to go to Algeria to show that French magic was superior to that of the Marabouts (a North African military/religious sect). This prevented them from rioting.

6. An American **Ehrich Weiss** (1874-1926) added an l to Houdin, the hero he had read about when a schoolboy, and became Houdini, the greatest escapologist of the time. He escaped from fetters, chains, prisons, boxes, ropes and even packing cases lowered into rivers covered in ice. Many of his tricks called for great courage, fitness and self-control. What appeared foolhardy were delicately balanced feats of skill combined with conjuring. He spent a considerable time

towards the end of his life exposing fraudulent mediums and denouncing spiritualism. One of his methods was to reproduce the medium's trick and often improve on it.

7. **John Nevil Maskelyne** (1839-1917) was an English magician, who invented many tricks and illusions. He founded a magic theatre in London, the Egyptian Hall, Piccadilly, London which he and his sons and grandsons ran for many years. It later moved to St George's Hall. He encouraged, engaged in and advised on the inventions of other magicians. It was he who in 1865 introduced the feat of escaping from a locked and roped box. In 1875 he 'levitated' a girl into the air without apparent support.

8. **David Wighton,** also English, (1868-1941) who called himself Devant, was one of John Maskelyne's partners. He became the greatest of conjurors and a remarkable magical inventor. He wrote several books on magic, such as 'Magic Made Easy', 'Lessons in Conjuring' and 'Woes of a Wizard'.

9. **Buatier de Kolta** (1845-1903), a Frenchman who appeared in many of Maskelyne's shows, invented some of the most striking magical effects ever. It was he who first made a girl appear to rise without support in the air, he would then cover her with a white sheet and when she had risen to some 7 feet he would snatch the sheet away and reveal – nothing. He also invented the vanishing bird cage and bird. The method used, which included the collapse of the hinged cage, often killed the bird. For this reason the RSPCA banned his method. If you see the trick today another method is used. It was he who invented 'Black Art', (see page 172).

10. **P. T. Selbit,** though little remembered outside the world of magicians, was the first in London in 1920 to saw a lady in half, the most commercially successful illusion ever invented.

11. The American **Howard Thurston** (1869-1936) is claimed by some to have been the greatest card manipulator ever. But he produced some spectacular illusions with cars, and a version of the Indian Rope trick. His show was spectacular. Although his apparatus alone took up some 10 railway carriages, he was at his finest with a simple pack of cards.

12. **Horace Goldin** (1873-1939) specialized in massive illusions requiring cumbersome apparatus but there was nothing cumbersome about his show. Illusion after illusion went by with dazzling and confusing speed. When he sawed a woman in half, he didn't just use a jobbing carpenter's saw,

nor did he conceal most of the girl with a box — she lay covered in nothing but a flimsy frock while he used a massive motor driven circular saw.

13. **Chung Ling Soo**, a New Yorker whose real name was William Robinson, will never be forgotten because of the horrifying manner of his death. On March 23, 1981, at the Wood Green Empire, London, Chung Ling Soo came to the climax of his show, the most dangerous of all illusions 'Defying the Bullets'.

    His routine was to load two guns with bullets marked by the audience. He then held a china plate over his heart and asked two members of a local rifle club to aim carefully at his heart and pull the triggers. On this occasion, there were the two normal gun shots and Chung Ling Soo took two paces forward, collapsed and died. The curtains closed at once making most of the audience think it was part of the show. At the inquest, Robert Churchill, the gun expert showed that the death was an accident. Some powder had trickled through into the wrong place and fired.

    When you next see this trick in a theatre or on TV remember that *at least* 8 skilled and experienced magicians have for one reason or another been killed performing it.

14. **David Nixon** who died at the end of the 1970s was, in common with all excellent conjurors and illusionists, inventive, creative and a fine builder of apparatus.

15. **Tommy Cooper,** who died in 1984, was not just a loveable bufoon of a conjuror, he was a skilled magician and capable of dazzling an audience by completing a trick when they least expected it.

16. **Paul Daniels** is a skilled all-rounder. His sleight of hand is second to none. His ability to misdirect his audience while performing an illusion is so good that skilled professional magicians are also taken in. He admits that he frequently re-thinks an old standby illusion or trick, not just for the audience but in order to get a kick out of fooling the professionals.

A Christmas list

1. **CHRISTMAS REINDEER.** The name of Father Christmas's 8 small reindeer are: Dasher, Dancer, Prancer, Vixent, Comet, Cupid, Donner and Blitzen.
2. **NATALIE.** A girl's name. This is derived from the Latin 'natale domini' meaning Christmas Day.
3. **FATHER CHRISTMAS.** The drawings that show Father Christmas as he is today complete with white beard, boots and red and white cloak were originated by Thomas Nast, an American caricaturist, in 1863.
4. **CHRISTMAS TREES.** Prince Albert, Queen Victoria's consort, is said to have introduced the Christmas Tree to the British Isles. The custom had been with us for many years before that. The Romans decorated trees centuries ago at the feast of Saturnalia (see number 8). Prince Albert was the man who introduced it to Buckingham Palace.
5. **SANTA CLAUS.** Father Christmas, Santa, Santa Claus or Saint Nicholas was in fact bishop of Myra in the 4th century. He is also the patron saint of children, virgins, sailors, thieves, pawnbrokers, Sicily, Greece and Russia.

6. **SINT NIKOLAAS.** The Feast of *Sint* Nikolaas in the Netherlands and elsewhere in parts of Europe is on December 6. It is a school holiday and presents are given to children.
7. **CHRISTMAS DAY.** Jesus was almost certainly not born on December 25. This date was fixed by the church in A.D. 336, because it was thought to be the date of the winter solstice.
8. **CHRISTMAS DECORATIONS.** The custom of Christmas decorations was oddly enough a hangover from the pre-Christian Roman Feast of Saturn, when their temples were decorated with evergreen (see also number 4). The Druids used mistletoe. The Saxons introduced holly and ivy because most other leaves had turned brown and the holly had the added attraction of red berries.
9. **XMAS.** Although widely disliked as a vulgarity, Xmas for Christmas is correct and not even an abbreviation, just a short version. It goes back to Old English. The Greek word for 'Christ' begins with the letter 'chi', or X. This is, however, used as an abbreviation in other words, such as Xian for Christian.
10. **CHRISTMAS CARDS.** There is some mystery about the first Christmas card because wood engravers in the Middle Ages produced special Christmas pictures; but in the accepted modern sense the first Christmas card probably originated in 1843. It was designed by J. C. Horsley for his friend Henry Cole. Printed on it were the words 'A Merry Christmas and a Happy New Year to You.' A test of 1,000 were put on the market and immediately sold out. The custom had started. Today over 1,000 million are sold each year.

A list of Smiths

Smith may be a common enough name, but there have been many uncommon Smiths as you will see from this list.

1. **George Joseph (Brides in the Bath) Smith** murdered three women (1912, 1913 and 1914) after they had made wills in his favour. He married them, waited for them to take a bath then grabbed their feet, pulled sharply and left them submerged until they drowned. If there is any humour in murder it may be had from the fact that he married his last victim in the town of Bath.

2. **Dodie Smith** started as an actress before writing her first and instantly successful play 'Autumn Crocus', followed by 'Dear Octopus' and many works including 'The Hundred and One Dalmations'.

3. **Joseph Smith,** founder of the Mormons, born at Sharon, Vermont, had his first 'call' as a prophet in 1820. An angel told him in 1823 that a hidden gospel was on golden plates. In 1827 these were delivered into his hands. He translated and published them, for which he was ridiculed, by 1830. The Church of the Latter-day Saints established its head-quarters in Ohio. Smith, who took many 'spiritual' wives, was shot in jail in 1844.

4. **William Smith** (1769-1839) was the founder of geology. He studied the strata of England and introduced the law whereby you can date strata by the fossils in them.

5. **Thomas Southwood Smith** (1788-1861) studied medicine and was a physician at the London Fever Hospital. He was outwardly conventional but when Jeremy Bentham left his body to Smith, he kept the skeleton fully clothed and took it to University College Hospital (where it still is) and for some years it sat at the head of the table for important meetings.

6. **William Henry Smith** (1792-1865) started a newsagents business in the Strand, London in 1812 and with his son, also W. H. Smith, was the first newsagent to use carts and trains to aid distribution. This helped him get the railway station concessions for selling books and papers.

7. **Augustus John Smith** was king of the Scilly Isles from 1857 until his death in 1872.

8. **John Stafford Smith** (1750-1836), an Englishman, wrote 'The Star-Spangled Banner'.

9. **Ian Douglas Smith** (1919-), Prime Minister of Rhodesia declared independence in 1965 despite many talks and conferences to avoid it. Meetings with Harold Wilson, British Premier, aboard HMS *Tiger* (1966) and *Fearless* (1968) off Gibraltar to try to prevent this failed.

10. **Madeleine Smith** stood trial in Edinburgh in 1857 for murder by arsenic of her lover Pierre L'Angelier. Her motive to be rid of him was that she had a more congenial suitor. She asked him for the return of some compromising letters but was refused. She had bought arsenic three times but her brilliant defence by John Inglis resulted in a verdict of 'Not Proven', a verdict allowed by Scottish law. She died of natural causes.

Accidents

1. More women than men come back from winter sports with broken bones.
2. Lightening strikes and kills 10 times more people after than before lunch.
3. A boating accident is 12 times more likely to kill you than a motor accident.
4. Banana skins generally get a bad press but a quick check of the casualty departments of 3 large hospitals reveals no records of any accidents due to slipping on banana skins.
5. Dead jellyfish sting. Accidently researched this myself.
6. If you are to be murdered, the odds are heavily in favour of your spouse doing it.
7. A baby was recently christened 'Encore' because he was not on the family programme.
8. Drab grey, green and blue cars are more likely to be involved in accidents than bright yellow, red and white cars.
9. To avoid being on a plane where a looney carries a bomb, Clement Freud, M.P. suggests carrying one yourself. The reason? The odds on being on a flight with one bomb are several millions to one against. But the odds on being on a flight with two bombs are so immense as to be incalculable. Seems to make sense.

A curious list of things people have done for no apparent reason

However remote the reason, most of us can see the point of climbing the world's highest mountain, exploring the deepest cave, running faster than anyone before, and so on, but there are records broken which seemingly lack logical motivation. In the 'Guinness Book of Records 1984' (Human Achievements) you will read:

1. 'The largest yo-yo ever constructed was one by Dr Tom Kuhn weighing 116.11 kg (256 lb) test launched from a 52 m (150 ft) crane in San Francisco on 13 October, 1979.'
2. 'Unsupported circle. The highest recorded number of people

who have demonstrated the physical paradox of all being seated without a chair in an unsupported circle is 10,323 employees of the Nissan Motor Company at Komasawa Stadium, Tokyo, Japan on 23 October, 1982.'

3. 'Pillar box standing. The record number of people to pile on top of a pillar box — oval top of 0.55 m square (6 sq feet) — is 29, all students of the City of London College, Moorgate, in Finsbury Circus, City of London on 21 October, 1971.'

4. 'Writing under handicap. The ultimate feat in "funny writing" would appear to be the ability to write extemporaneously and decipherably backwards, upside down, laterally inverted (mirror style) while blindfolded with both hands simultaneously. Three claims to this ability with both hands and feet simultaneously, by Mrs Carolyn Webb of Thirlmere, NSW, Australia, Mrs Judy Hall of Chesterfield, Virginia, USA, and Robert Gray of Toronto, Ontario, Canada, are outstanding but have yet to be witnessed by our staff.'

5. 'Spinning. The duration record for spinning a metal top by hand is 12 minutes 44 seconds by Peter Hodgson, Southend-on-Sea on 28 May, 1984.'

6. 'String ball largest. The largest ball of string on record is one of 3.88 m (12 ft 9 in) in diameter, 12.19 m (40 ft) in circumference and weighing 10 tons amassed by Francis A. Johnson of Darwin, Minnesota, USA, between 1950-78.'

7. 'Egg dropping. The greatest height from which fresh eggs have been dropped (to earth) and remained intact is 198 m (650 ft) by David S. Donoghue from a helicopter on 2 October, 1979 on a Tokyo Golf Course.'

8. 'Hoop rolling. In 1968 it was reported that Zolilio Diaz (Spain) had rolled a hoop 965 km (600 miles) from Mieres to Madrid and back in 18 days.'

9. 'Clapping. The duration record for continuous clapping (sustaining an average of 140 claps per minute audible at 91 m (100 yd) is 50 hours 17 minutes by Ashrita Furman of Jamaica, New York, USA on 10-12 August, 1981.'

10. 'Golf ball balancing. Lang Martin balanced 7 golf balls vertically without adhesive at Charlotte, North Carolina, USA on 9 February, 1980.'

Japanese monster films

Before you get ambitions to make a monster film, take a look at some of the monsters invented by Japanese film makers:

1. **Doroga**   Huge jellyfish.
2. **Ebirah**   Enormous shrimp.
3. **Gammera**   A turtle as big as an aircraft carrier.
4. **Gappa**   A huge lizard.
5. **Godzilla**   54 metres (165 ft) high Tyrannosaurus Rex.
6. **Goke**   A vampire.
7. **Gorag**   An enormous flesh eating reptile.
8. **Gyaos**   A fox with dazzling cunning and exceptional brain.
9. **Hedorah**   A smog monster.
10. **Mantanga**   A corrupting fungus which grows and grows.
11. **Mothra**   A giant moth.
12. **Rodan**   A terrifyingly huge pterodactyl.
13. **Varan**   An enormous rat.
14. **Viras**   A titanic squid.

It hardly needs saying all are bent on man's destruction.

Eating and drinking records

The Guinness Book of Records warns that trying to establish such records is *'extremely inadvisable, particularly among young people'*. With that warning not to emulate the gutsy, here goes! Specific records have been claimed as follows:

1. **Baked beans.** 2,780 cold baked beans one by one with a cocktail stick in 30 minutes by Karen Stevenson of Wallasey, Merseyside on 4 April, 1981.
2. **Beer drinking while upsidedown.** 2 pints – 6.4 seconds by Peter Dowdeswell at the Top Rank Club, Northants.
3. **Chicken.** 1.701 kg (3 lb 12 oz) in 12 minutes 37 seconds by Shaun Barry, East Molesey, Surrey on 26 January, 1984.
4. **Kippers.** 27 (which she also filleted) in 60 minutes by Karen Stevenson of Wallasey, Merseyside on 5 March, 1982.
5. **Meat.** One whole roast ox in 42 days by Johann Ketzler of Munich, Germany in 1980.

6. **Pancakes** 15.2 cm (6 inch) diameter buttered and with syrup. 62 in 6 minutes 58.5 seconds by Peter Dowdeswell at The Drapery, Northampton on 9 February, 1977.
7. **Prunes.** 144 in 35 seconds by Peter Dowdeswell, Lowestoft, Suffolk on 25 September, 1983.
8. **Snails.** 1 kg (35.27 oz) in 3 minutes 45.78 seconds by the same Peter Dowdeswell (see also Prunes and Beer) at Hever Castle, Kent on 27 June 1984.
9. **Tree.** 3.35 m (11 ft) birch, 12 cm (4.7 in) diameter trunk. In 89 hours by Jay Gwaltney, 19 on WKQX's, 'Outrageous Contest', Chicago, U.S.A., 11-15 September, 1980.
10. **Greatest Omnivore.** Michel Lolito (b. 1950) of Grenoble, France, known as Monsieur Mangetout, has been eating metal and glass since 1959. Gastroenterologists have X-rayed his stomach but remain mystified. His diet since 1966 has included seven bicycles, a supermarket trolley in 4½ days, 7 TV sets and a low calorie Cessna light aircraft which he ate in Caracas, Venezuela.

Landmarks in the advent of the computer

1. No one knows when the first computer, the *abacus*, was invented or who was the inventor. It was in use well before 5,000 B.C. and is still used widely today in parts of China, Japan and Eastern Europe. It can calculate with and 'remember' small numbers very well.
2. John Napier (1550-1617), a Scottish inventor, simplified division by explaining it in terms of a series of subtractions, and multiplication by a series of additions. In 1617 he described methods of doing multiplication and division with bones. This, combined with original data tables, was a great contribution to mechanical computing. (See under BRITISH BORN INVENTORS, page 42.)
3. In 1642 Blaise Pascal, the French philosopher, built a calculating machine by linking toothed wheels together, so that the first wheel on the right showed units, the next showed tens and so on, rather like electricity and gas meters in use today. Modestly, he called his invention *Le Pascaline*.

4. In 1671 Gottfried Leibniz (1646-1716), a German philosopher and mathematician, invented the *Stepped Reckoner*, similar to, but more advanced than '*Le Pascaline*' in that it could multiply, divide and give square roots. A working model was demonstrated to the Royal Society in London, but found to be unreliable.

5. Charles Babbage (1792-1871), Professor of Mathematics at Cambridge University, has been called the inventor of the modern computer, although strictly speaking his machine was nowhere near the computers of today. In 1835 he came up with his 'Analytical Machine' which could combine arithmetical processes with decisions based on its own computation. The machine used a system of punched cards and 50 counter wheels.

6. Recent evidence shows that a great deal of the glory of Babbage's machine should be shared with Lord Byron's only legitimate daughter, Countess Ada Lovelace. She had a superb mathematical brain and without her help the machine would never had been built. It was she who wrote programs for it and was therefore the first computer programmer.

7. In 1859 George Boole, the English mathematician, wrote about the binary system. That is to say he advocated the use of 0 to mean OFF and 1 to mean ON. Most computers today use this system because it is easier to make a switch which is either ON or OFF rather than have (say) a *decimal* switch with 10 positions.

8. In the early 1800s the Jacquard loom used punched holes to control the pattern of the weave.

9. In 1886 Herman Hollerith, (1860-1929), an American administrator, who was working on a US census, enlarged on the punched card system by allowing needles to fall through the holes and into little cups of mercury to complete an electrical circuit, so that *sensing* was automatic. This was faster than handwritten tally sheets. The computer as we know it was getting closer.

10. Valdemar Poulsen (1869-1942), a Danish electrical engineer, invented magnetic recording in 1900. In those days it was on fast running steel wire, the forerunner of the iron oxide emulsion, brown plastic tape. This allowed information to be stored magnetically. His wire recorder created great interest at the Paris Exposition of 1900.

11. That vital switch mentioned in number 7, but not then devised, appeared in the form of a valve called an electronic switch and was the creation of Lee de Forest (1873-1961), an American inventor, in 1906.
12. The first electro-mechanical computer was built in Buckinghamshire during the 1939-45 war by a team led by Alan Turing, an English mathematician (1912-1954). The huge machine, called Colossus, contained over 1,500 valves, some of which would burn out every few minutes.
13. In 1947 came the silicon transistor, which replaced the unreliable valves in radios and, more importantly, in computers. These transistors do not heat up and can be switched on and off at high speed without breaking down.
14. In the 1960s circuit designs were miniaturized and printed on to silicon chips. Different circuits could be printed on to many different chips. Combinations of these chips brought about the invention of the microprocessor incorporated in the microcomputers now seen in all large businesses, many schools and in even more homes.
15. The future? Computers have already been designed to recognise voices, to 'see' and recognize faces, to speak cheerfully to a smiling face and not so cheerfully to a face that looks worried. Three dimensional computer pictures are already used for examining terrain from space, for computer games, for industrial design. So where to now? The prospect of a computer that can program itself is already in view.

Origins of words

ALPHABET   Direct combination of the first two letters of the Greek alphabet – *alpha* and *beta*.

CHORTLE   Coined by Lewis Carroll in *'Through the Looking-Glass'* where he combines *chuckle* with *snort*.

QUINTESSENCE   To the four elements: earth, fire, water and air the Greeks added the fifth or *quint* element to form the basis of the stars.

TANTALIZE   Derives from one Tantalus, a mythological Greek king who was punished by Zeus. Tantalus was immersed in water with fruit above his head. When he reached for the fruit it rose out of reach, and when he tried to drink, the water would recede.

BEDLAM   A mad house from a corruption of Bethlehem. The priory of St Mary of Bethlehem was an asylum for the insane from 1377 near London's Bishopsgate. In 1676 they were all moved to Moorfields where they became one of the sights of London. Entrance fee for the morbid viewer was twopence.

SOPHOMORE   Greek *SOPHOS* meaning wise, with *MOROS* meaning foolish. One who is half wise and half foolish.

PIGGYBACK   Carrying a pack on your back was known as *pick-a-pack*. It was corrupted to *piggyback* by children.

PANDEMONIUM   Invented by John Milton in *Paradise Lost*. He took it from the Greek word *pan* meaning all, and *daimon* a demon. Hell was viewed as a place of uproar and confusion.

SUPERCILIOUS   This means characterizing scorn. Scornful people often raise the eyebrows. It is from the Latin *super* meaning above and *cilium* an eyelid.

TAWDRY   On the feast day of St Audrey cheap lace and other articles of dress were sold. The quality was so poor they were known as *Staudrey* and slowly the word became *tawdry*.

A handy list of weights and measures

We are asked to talk in litres, but milk and beer are usually delivered in **pints**. Most of us still buy petrol in **gallons**, not litres, and ask how many **miles**, not kilometres, it is from here to there. The corner shop greengrocer looks blank if you ask him for 2.265 kilos of potatoes instead of 5 pounds. Yet the Post Office insists on the normal letter weighing under 60 grams and likes medium-sized envelopes which measure 203 millimetres × 120 millimetres. To understand all this **instantly** is too much for most of us, so to help you, here are some conversion tables.

LITRES		PINTS/ GALLONS	PINTS/ GALLONS		LITRES
1	about	1¾ pints	1 pint	about	0.57
2	about	3½ pints	2 pints	about	1.15
3	about	5¼ pints	4 pints	about	2.3
4	about	7 pints	6 pints	about	3.41
5	about	1.1 gallons	1 gallon	about	4.5
6	about	1.3 gallons	2 gallons	about	9.1
7	about	1.5 gallons	3 gallons	about	13.6
8	about	1.8 gallons	4 gallons	about	18.2
9	about	2 gallons	5 gallons	about	22.7
10	about	2.2 gallons	6 gallons	about	27.3
20	about	4.4 gallons	7 gallons	about	31.8
30	about	6.6 gallons	8 gallons	about	36.4
40	about	8.8 gallons	9 gallons	about	40.9
50	about	11.0 gallons	10 gallons	about	45.5

A quick way to convert kilometres to miles is to divide the kilometres by 8 and multiply by 5, and to convert miles to kilometres divide by 5 and multiply by 8.

KILOMETRES		MILES	MILES		KILOMETRES
		(These are all approximate)			
1	=	0.625	1	=	1.6
3	=	1.875	3	=	4.8
5	=	3.125	5	=	8.05
10	=	6.25	10	=	16.0
15	=	9.375	15	=	24.0
20	=	12.5	20	=	32.35
30	=	18.75	30	=	48.25
40	=	25.0	40	=	64.4
50	=	31.0	50	=	80.5
100	=	62.0	100	=	161

CENTIMETRES		INCHES/FEET	INCHES/FEET		CENTIMETRES
1	=	0.4 inch	1 inch	=	2.5
5	=	2 inches	3 inches	=	7.5
10	=	4 inches	6 inches	=	15.0
20	=	8 inches	9 inches	=	22.5
50	=	1 ft 8 in	1 foot	=	30.5
75	=	2 ft 6 in	2 ft	=	61.0
100	=	3 ft 3 in	3 ft	=	91.5
			(1 metre)		

GRAMS		OUNCES	OUNCES		GRAMS
10	=	0.35	½	=	14
50	=	1.75	1	=	28
100	=	3.5	2	=	56
125	=	4.25	5	=	142
500	=	1 lb 1½ oz	12	=	340
1000	=	2 lb 3 oz	16	=	453
(1 kilo)			(1 lb)		

Confusion reigns when a citizen of the USA meets, for instance, a Frenchman who uses the Grams/Kilos system and a Scot who uses pounds and stones. There are problems when they discuss their own weights.

The man from the USA says he weighs 140 lb, the Frenchman says he weighs 63.5 kilos and the Scot says he weighs 10 stone. They get on the scales to see what all this means and discover they all weigh the same.

STONES		POUNDS		KILOS
1	=	14	=	6.35
7	=	98	=	44.5
8	=	112	=	51
9	=	126	=	57
10	=	140	=	63.5
11	=	154	=	70
12	=	168	=	76
13	=	182	=	82.5
14	=	196	=	89
15	=	210	=	95

A list mainly of epitaphs

Author and publishers do not vouch for the authenticity of all of them.

1. It is said that a hypochondriac insisted that his tombstone should read:
'I TOLD YOU SO'.
2. This was written by Benjamin Franklin for himself but was not used on his tombstone:
'THE BODY OF BENJAMIN FRANKLIN, PRINTER (LIKE THE COVER OF AN OLD BOOK, ITS CONTENTS TORN OUT AND STRIPPED OF ITS LETTERING AND GILDING), LIES HERE, FOOD FOR WORMS; BUT THE WORK SHALL NOT BE LOST, FOR IT WILL (AS HE BELIEVED) APPEAR ONCE MORE IN A NEW AND MORE ELEGANT EDITION REVISED AND CORRECTED BY THE AUTHOR.'

3. Boswell wrote that Samuel Johnson said:
   'THE WRITER OF AN EPITAPH SHOULD NOT BE CONSIDERED AS
   SAYING NOTHING BUT WHAT IS STRICTLY TRUE. ALLOWANCE
   MUST BE MADE FOR SOME DEGREE OF EXAGGERATED PRAISE.
   IN LAPIDARY INSCRIPTIONS A MAN IS NOT UPON OATH.'

4. David McCord, Epitaph on a Waiter:
   'BY AND BY
   GOD CAUGHT HIS EYE.'
5. Jessica Mitford in *The American Way of Death* reported this
   inscription on a man's tombstone by his widow:
   'REST IN PEACE — UNTIL WE MEET AGAIN.'
6. Said to be on a tombstone in Birmingham:
   'HERE LIES THE MOTHER OF CHILDREN SEVEN,
   FOUR ON EARTH AND THREE IN HEAVEN;
   THE THREE IN HEAVEN PREFERRING RATHER
   TO DIE WITH MOTHER THAN LIVE WITH FATHER.'
7. Should you be in Covent Garden Church, look for this one, an
   epitaph to the highwayman Claude DuVall:
   'HERE LIES DUVALL; READER IF MALE THOU ART,
   LOOK TO THY PURSE; IF FEMALE TO THY HEART.'
8. Alexander Pope wrote this:
   'FRIEND, IN YOUR EPITAPH I'M GRIEVED
   SO VERY MUCH IS SAID:
   ONE HALF WILL NEVER BE BELIEVED.
   THE OTHER NEVER READ.

9. This can be seen in the Parish Church, Bury St. Edmunds on the stone over the grave of printer:
'LIKE A WORN OUT TYPE, HE IS RETURNED TO THE FOUNDER IN THE HOPE OF BEING RECAST IN A BETTER AND MORE PERFECT MOULD.'

10. Woody Allen said 'I'm not afraid of dying. I just don't want to be around when it happens.'

11. W.C. Fields is reported to have asked for this epitaph:
'ON THE WHOLE I'D RATHER BE IN PHILADELPHIA.'

12. Memorial to Mrs Alfred White (weight 22 stone):
'OPEN WIDE YE PEARLY GATES
THAT LEAD TO THE HEAVENLY SHORE;
OUR FATHER SUFFERED PASSING THROUGH
AND MOTHER WEIGHS MUCH MORE.'

13. To the sacred memory of George Bates who died August 6, 1800:
'HIS WIDOW, AGED 24, LIVES AT 7 ELM STREET, HAS EVERY QUALIFICATION FOR A GOOD WIFE, AND YEARNS TO BE COMFORTED.'

14. This can be seen in Church Stretton (Salop):
'ON A THURSDAY SHE WAS BORN,
ON A THURSDAY MADE A BRIDE,
ON A THURSDAY PUT TO BED,
ON A THURSDAY BROKE HER LEG,
AND
ON A THURSDAY DIED.'

15. In a Grantham (Lincs) Churchyard over a sexton's grave:
'I, THAT HAVE CARRIED A HUNDRED BODIES BRAVE,
AM BY A FEVER CARRIED TO MY GRAVE;
I CARRIED, AND AM CARRIED, SO THAT'S EVEN;
MAY I BE A PORTER TO THE GATES OF HEAVEN.'

16. In Minster churchyard, Ripon, Yorkshire.
'HERE LIES POOR BUT HONEST BRYAN TUNSTAL;
HE WAS AN EXCELLENT ANGLER UNTIL
DEATH, ENVIOUS OF HIS MERIT,
THREW OUT HIS LINE, HOOKED HIM,
AND LANDED HIM HERE. THE 21ST DAY OF APRIL 1970.'

17. From a rural district in the Midlands:
'BENEATH THESE STONES REPOSE THE BONES
OF THEODOSIUS GRIM;
HE DRANK HIS BEER FROM YEAR TO YEAR,
UNTIL THE BIER TOOK HIM.'

18. Thomas Alleyn was buried with his two wives in 1650 with this thoughtful inscription on their common tombstone:
'DEATH HERE ADVANTAGE HATH OF LIFE I SPYE,
ONE HUSBAND WITH TWO WIVES AT ONCE MAY LYE.'

19. To be seen in Bath Abbey:
'HERE LIES ANN MANN;
SHE LIVED AN OLD MAID AND DIED AN OLD MAN.'

20. Merideth was an organist at St Mary Winton College, Oxford. This is still to be seen over his grave:
'HERE LIES ONE BLOWN OUT OF BREATH,
WHO LIVED A MERRY LIFE, AND DIED A MERIDETH.'

21. From an architect's grave in Gateshead churchyard, Durham,
'HERE LIES ROBERT TROLLOP
WHO MADE YON STONES ROLL UP;
WHEN DEATH TOOK HIS SOUL UP,
HIS BODY FILLED THIS HOLE UP.'

22. This well-known epitaph to that most competent of lawyers, Sir John Strange, is worth quoting even at the risk of repetition:
'HERE LIES AN HONEST LAWYER,
AND THAT IS STRANGE.'

23. In Poole churchyard, Dorset, a very tall man called Day is buried:
'AS LONG AS LONG CAN BE,
SO LONG SO LONG WAS HE;
HOW LONG, HOW LONG, DOST SAY?
AS LONG AS THE LONGEST DAY.'

24. In a Sheffield churchyard you may see this:
'BENEATH THESE STONES
LIES WILLIAM JONES,
THE BAILIFF AND THE BUM;
WHEN HE DIED
THE DEVIL CRIED
"COME BILLY, COME." '

25. In Sevenoaks, Parish church, Kent may still be seen:
'GRIM DEATH TOOK ME WITHOUT ANY WARNING
I WAS WELL AT NIGHT, AND DIED IN THE MORNING.'

26. In Westminster Abbey this can still be seen, and possibly written by John Gay (Beggar's Opera) himself for his own epitaph:
'LIFE IS A JEST, AND ALL THINGS SHOW IT;
I THOUGHT SO ONCE AND NOW I KNOW IT.'

27. One Susan Blake asked Sir Thomas More to write her epitaph which he did, like this:
'GOOD SUSAN BLAKE IN ROYAL STATE
ARRIVED AT LAST AT HEAVEN'S GATE.'
Some years elapsed and the two had a quarrel over something unrecorded, after which Sir Thomas added:
'BUT PETER MET HER WITH A CLUB
AND KNOCKED HER BACK TO BEELZEBUB.'

28. This one is from Falkirk churchyard:
'AT REST BENEATH THIS SLAB OF STONE,
LIES STINGY JIMMY WYETT,
HE DIED ONE MORNING JUST AT TEN
AND SAVED A DINNER BY IT.'

29. Near Stroud, Gloucestershire, is the village of Painswick. Look in the churchyard to find this:
'MY WIFE IS DEAD, AND HERE SHE LIES,
NOBODY LAUGHS AND NOBODY CRIES;
WHERE SHE'S GONE AND HOW SHE FARES,
NOBODY KNOWS, AND NOBODY CARES.'

30. A doubtful one supposedly from Oxfordshire:
'HERE LIES THE BODY OF JOHN ELDRED,
AT LEAST, HE WILL BE HERE WHEN HE'S DEAD;
BUT NOW AT THIS TIME HE IS ALIVE,
THE 14TH OF AUGUST, SIXTY FIVE.'

31. This incredible inscription is in Cheltenham:
'HERE LIES I AND MY TWO DAUGHTERS,
KILLED BY DRINKING CHELTENHAM WATERS;
IF WE HAD STUCK TO EPSOM SALTS,
WE'D NOT BE LYING IN THESE HERE VAULTS.'

32. Dr Walker, the author of 'English Particles' has this enlightening information on his tombstone:
'HERE LIES WALKER'S PARTICLES.'

33. Odd though it reads, this can still be seen in the Irish churchyard at Belturbet:
'HERE LIES JOHN HIGLEY, WHOSE MOTHER AND FATHER WERE DROWNED IN THEIR PASSAGE FROM AMERICA. HAD THEY BOTH LIVED THEY WOULD HAVE BEEN BURIED HERE.'

34. I would like my own epitaph to be:
'THAT'S MY LOT.'